West Meets East

West Meets East

A Primer On The
Israeli/Palestinian Conflict

David Harb

Library of Congress Control Number:		2010912519
ISBN:	Hardcover	978-1-4535-6359-5
	Softcover	978-1-4535-6358-8
	Ebook	978-1-4535-6360-1

To order additional copies of this book, contact:
Xlibris Corporation
1-888-795-4274
www.Xlibris.com
Orders@Xlibris.com
82858

Contents

Dedication

This book is dedicated to Audi Rontisi family of Ramallah (fourteen miles north of Jerusalem). Audi and his lovely wife Patricia ran an orphanage home in Ramallah for forty years. They have a beautiful daughter, Hillary. Hillary is a graduate of Harvard University, and she is currently on staff as a specialist in the Middle East studies program.

Acknowledgements

It is impossible to acknowledge all that have encouraged me to write this book. There are so many. I must thank Barbara Aces of Xlibris Publishing for her unending help and assistance. Also Faith Go, Alice Rynaud and the entire staff at Xlibris.

I must thank my sisters Martha and Peggy for their continuous support and encouragement over all these years. They never gave up on me. Thanks to All my friends on Fripp Island; especially Rev. Jerry Hammond and Joe Wreen. Joe is the best listener I have ever known. He has more knowledge of the Ocean and it's depths than any person I have know. On so many of our fishing trips, Joe has given me so much advice about my book. Thank you Joe.

Pastor Mark at Sea Side Vineyards Church has helped me continue when I wanted to quit. Thank you Mark. My friends at the Preserve in Port Royal, especially Marine Officer Clark Phillips. I can't leave out Gail Werde. Gail is the most positive man I have ever met. He was so posivite, even during his chemotherapy treatments. Gail has more character than any one I have ever known. He just would not stop encouraging me.

To all my friends in Atlanta, too many to mention, I say thank you. Howard Kasow of Marathon, Fla. Has been much more than a listener and friend. He has also been patient and kind. Lastly but not the least, all of you in California.

I am truly blessed to have so many friends that have unselfishly helped me complete this book.

Foreword

What do you want? How bad do you want it? Are you willing to pay the price? This book is not intended to be crammed with power phrases that you've heard a thousand times. Rather, it is intended to empower you to do something about what you've read.

We are dealing with a vital topic; the Middle East—specifically, the Palestine/Israel conflict.

Just how important is it to resolve this conflict? Consider this: Before he was elected president, Barak Obama was viewed internationally as one of the most phenomenal persons in our history. After he was elected, the whole world was watching to see what he would do relative to the Middle East Situation.

What did President Obama do on his first day in office? Some of you remember vividly what he did. Most of you heard what he did, because it was broadcast by every network in the United States and most media sources around the world, but have you forgotten? Too many of us, unfortunately, do not have a clue.

On President Obama's first day in the office, his number one agenda was the Palestine/Israel conflict. He spent the day on the telephone. He called the president of Egypt. He called the president of the Palestinian Authority. He called the prime minister of Israel. Of all the conflicts around the world, and there are many, the most important agenda for the president of the United States of America on his first day in office was the Palestine/Israel conflict. If you doubt this, I challenge you to Google what the president did on his first day in office and prove it for yourself.

Why is solving this conflict so important? We can go back to as early as 1950 and read some of the headlines. There was talk then that the issue was so hot it could escalate into World War III.

President Obama spent his first day in office contacting the leadership to the Israeli/Palestinian conflict. It was his first agenda. This is an important issue. I'm not trying to be an alarmist. I am simply trying to inform the reader of the importance of this issue. If you arm yourself with the facts, you can become a potent person in helping to bring peace to the Middle East conflict.

In addressing the *Palestine/Israel* conflict, I refer to Palestine first, not because I want this book to have a pro-Palestinian bias, but simply because we have been conditioned by referring to it as the Israel/Palestine conflict. It isn't that Israel is the winner and Palestine is the loser or that Israel is the loser and Palestine is the winner.

Isn't it interesting? If we just change the order of those two words perhaps, we will perhaps begin to see the conflict from a different perspective. This is what I'm trying to do *vis-a-vis* educating the reader.

Remember the Rodney King issue? It was a case where police were chasing a car that wouldn't obey their command to pull over. They finally overcame him, and their own cameras recorded several police beating on him. All the TV networks picked up on it. Every network was showing videos of police brutally beating on a man. People were screaming police brutality. The incident polarized America. Riots broke out. We finally came back to our senses when Rodney King spoke those memorable words, "Can't we get along?"

The similar awaking can happen with the Palestine/Israel conflict. There can be peace. There will be peace. That is the purpose of this book. Don't lose sight of this. You will miss the point unless you are to have an open mind. Don't get bogged down with finger pointing.

Who am I trying to reach with this book? Who is my audience? What am I trying to say? Where do I begin? Trying to get a grasp on these questions is not a simple undertaking. It is a formidable task. It is something that I have been wrestling with for the past forty years, but, somehow, there must be a beginning. Let's get on with it.

My audience includes the following

- Christian Church in America
- The voting public
- Jewish community in America.
- Arab community in America
- All Americans interested in peace
- Not just America, but all countries interested in Middle East

There is a strong need for the Christians and the Jews in this country to have an open dialogue on the Middle East issue. We do not need to politicize these issues in the church. Rather, the church has a responsibility to argue for justice and educate its congregation on the injustice that is taking place in Palestine/ Israel, especially the persecution of Christians in the region.

The Jewish community in America needs to see how they have turned a blind eye to the atrocities that are being committed by the government in Israel.

What I am trying to say is that there can be peace, but a few heads have to be turned. This book is about turning heads in the right direction—the direction towards peace.

Chapter 1

Destroying the Myth

The prevailing myth is: "Those Arabs and Jews have been fighting for over four thousand years. It is senseless and useless for anyone who attempts to stop them in engaging in their continuous fighting. It is an exercise of complete futility."

The interesting thing about a myth is that if you hear it repeated often enough, it begins to take on the character of truth. You hear it enough times, and it begins to sound like the truth. Pretty soon, you hear it from someone else, and now, it is beginning to become widespread and you have heard it so many times that you can repeat it. Bingo! You have now bought into the myth! To you, it is the truth. But is it? Let's examine the facts.

The facts can be proven both biblically and historically. If you are willing to look at the biblical facts, we can cut the myth in half. If we go back two thousand years, it was the time of Jesus Christ.

At that time, all of Palestine was under Roman Occupation. Any resistance by either the Arabs or the Jews was quickly brought under control by the tight grip and power of the Roman government.

The Jews were not fighting the Arabs; they were showing all of their resistance against the Roman Occupation. The Romans were expelling all the Jews from Rome.

After the crucifixion of Christ, the Romans turned to expelling the Jews from Palestine. In AD 70, the Jews put up one of the fiercest fights in all history. They were determined and proud, (they are to this day) but the power of the Roman Army was too great. Even so, they wouldn't give up. Historians have recorded the greatest of this as the Bar Kochba revolt in AD 132. It was so horrible and bloody that at the beginning of each day you could hear groaning and screams of the fighting the night before, and there were so many bodies all over that you could not see the streets. Starvation was so horrible that women were reported to have roasted their children for food.

The history of Masada shows that the Jews were so determined no t to be taken by the Romans that about nine hundred made a suicide pact. They carried it out, and all died except one to record the horrible event.

We all need to show compassion and love for the suffering of the Jews at that horrible time in their history. However, let's not confuse the facts of history. The Jews were not fighting the Arabs. They were fighting the Romans. After AD 125, almost all of the Jews were dispersed (diaspora) from Palestine.

Are we beginning to dispel the myth? I hardly think so. Old myths are hard to dispel. But given enough facts, the truth repeated enough times, any myth can be destroyed. Let's continue.

In the Fifteenth century, the Turks (Ottoman Empire) began to occupy Palestine. The Ottoman (Turkish) Period (1517-1917).

In 1517, Selim I (the Grim) of Turkey defeated the Mamelukes and took over Palestine. Even prior to this, the Ottoman Turks (named after the Sultan Osman I) had taken over Constantinople in 1453. From there, they ruled Palestine. The son of Selim I was Selyman (also called Subeiman), the magnificent. He ruled from 1520-1566 and was their greatest monarch during the four-hundred-year Turkish occupation of Palestine. Most of the Jews were gone, so they weren't fighting the Palestinians. So far, we've cut the myth from four thousand years to five hundred years. Let's continue. Among Subeiman's other achievements, he rebuilt the walls of Jerusalem, which stand today as a monument to his greatness. Soon after his death, the land was ruled by a number of pashas (provincial governors of Turkish birth). They paid the Turkish government in Constantinople huge bribes to rule over certain parts of the Middle East. This really began the era of the "Abominable Turk." With few exceptions, Palestine was now ruled over by a group of greedy, dense, and cruel tax collectors, who raped both people and land. Jews, Arabs, and Christians, all suffered equally under their disgraceful rule.

In 1798, Napoleon Bonaparte entered the Middle East. During that year, he captured Egypt with thirty thousand troops and a large fleet of ships. He then announced his intention to conquer Palestine and restore to the Jews this fatherland. Because of this, many Jews looked upon him as their true Messiah, an honor they had last paid some 665 years prior to Bar Kochba.

Napoleon then marched north along the Maritime plain and conquered Gaza, Jaffa, and Caesarea. At this time, he demonstrated some of his cruelty, murdering over three thousand prisoners of war at Jaffa on the beach, claiming he could find no other way to dispose of them. A Turkish army attempted to repulse him in the Jezreel Valley, but he defeated them at the foot of Mt. Tabor. But Napoleon could not take the strong central city of Acre. This coastal metropolis was defended by both the Turks and the British. Had he captured Acre, history would doubtless have been changed. The famous French emperor then set sail for home, never to return.

In 1838, the British Consulate opened in Jerusalem, the first of its kind. In 1843, France, Prussia, Austria, and Spain had done the same. The great European powers now became very interested in Palestine. Protestants, Catholics, and Jews also founded missions during this time. The Jewish population began slowly to rise. In 1839, there were 12,000, Jews; in 1880, 35,000; in 1900, 70,000, and by 1914, there were 90,000.

The Crimean War of 1853 was fought over the rights to Palestine. It began when Russia invaded Turkey to wrest some control from the Ottoman Empire at Constantinople concerning the Holy Land. Turkey turned to France and England for help. Russia lost that war.

The most significant event of the four-hundred-year Turkish rule, and indeed in Holy Land history since Bar-Kochba's AD 135 revolt, occurred in 1897. It was during that year that Theodor Herzl, an Austrian Jew, launched a political movement in Basel, Switzerland, known as Zionism. Two hundred and four delegates from Europe, Africa, America, and Palestine attended this momentous meeting which began on August 29. From this day, there emerged the world Zionist organization.

Herzl cried out: "There is a land without a people! There are a people without a land!" (This was not true; there were 1000s of Palestinians living there.) "Give the land without a people to the people without a land!" This mantra continued for years. It has been recorded that Golda Mier repeated it many times. For most well-intentioned, but uninformed Jews, it was the gospel.

Of course, this was not true. There were over a million Palestinians living there at the time. This is an excellent example of how myths get started. It sounded good, but it just wasn't true. Nevertheless, the seeds for conflict were planted, and it was music in the ears of those European Jews that were trying to survive in an almost impossible condition. Hated by the world, a dream of a land they could call their own must have sounded wonderfully good.

Immediately after the conference, Herzl launched into a program of ceaseless diplomatic efforts and negotiations with governmental leaders throughout Europe and western Asia. He visited Russia, Great Britain, Italy, Germany and talked with the Pope. He then went to Constantinople to see the Turkish Sultan himself, who controlled Palestine. G. Frederick Owen describes this amazing meeting:

> For months he sought the privilege of a personal interview with this grand ruler. Then one day, while Herzl sat waiting in the outer office, one of Sultan's many slaves

entered and beckoned the distinguished-looking man to follow him. They walked through the long and spacious corridors and finally arrived at the throne room. The room was decorated with many precious gems, and the Sultan's throne was of pure gold. Tall, dignified, handsome Theodor Herzl made a low, respectful bow, and began to speak as only Herzl could speak.

The Jews, he said, were persecuted everywhere in Europe, and could not seem to find a home anywhere but in America, which could not take them all. Would the Sultan consider letting them return to Palestine, their ancient homeland? While the small, round, gorgeously clothed Sultan sat on the soft pillows on his golden throne and listened, he was sufficiently impressed with this tall, handsome, eloquent visitor that he decorated him for his personal heroism and offered to permit the Jews to return to Palestine for twenty million dollars! Humanly speaking, this was the greatest opportunity afforded for the Jews in thirty centuries, since the days of Solomon, when they owned and controlled the Holy Land. But it was not to be. Herzl could persuade neither rich Jew nor Gentile to commit even a fraction of this human sales price. The golden opportunity soon faded forever. On July 3, 1904, Theodor Herzl died of a heart attack. He had, however, created a mighty wave of determination out on the stormy sea of Judaism which would increase in intensity, not to be stopped until it crashed heavily upon the shores of Palestine.

By the end of the nineteenth century, hostility against the abominable Turks was growing in Palestine.

In 1912, a discontented Turkish element organized a revolt called the Young Turk revolution. The Arabs supported this, hoping for a better rule, but soon found their new masters were as corrupt as the old ones were.

In the summer of 1914, an event took place which would forever change the political and geographical tapestry in the Middle East. It occurred on June 28 in Serbia when the Archduke Ferdinand (nephew and heir of the Austrian emperor) was shot and killed.

Austria and Germany almost immediately declared war on Serbia.
Russia came to help Serbia, along with Britain, France, and Italy.
Turkey sided in with Germany on November 5, 1914. But on June
9, 1916, the Arabs revolted against the Turks. They were aided in
this by Thomas E. Lawrence, a former British archaeologist, who
would later gain world fame as Lawrence of Arabia. He helped
raise an army of two-hundred-thousand Arabs to fight on the side
of Great Britain. With the aid of these two-hundred-thousand Arab
freedom fighters, (not terrorists), the British army won the war
against the Turks, and Great Britain became the "new" occupier!

The Ottoman Empire occupation of Palestine lasted for
over four hundred years. There were practically no Jews (only a
remnant) in Palestine, so obviously the Jews couldn't be fighting
the Palestinians.

The British occupation was short lived, however. For whatever
reason she decided that she could not colonize the Palestinian
people, Britain decided to turn over the question of Palestine to the
United Nations. The United Nations divided Palestine according to
what was to be called the partition plan and basically, it was half
for Israel and half for Palestine. (The Green line) The Palestinians
were not willing to give up half their land, and they went to war
in 1948 to recapture it. Of course, they were trounced, but that's
not the point here. The point here is 1948 is a more accurate date
of the beginning of the conflict.

The Israel/Palestinian conflict is just over sixty years old. They
have not been fighting for four thousand years.

This is a very simplistic explanation, and volumes have been
written to cover the periods I have lightly covered. If my readers
can just accept the fact that I am trying to convey that the myth
(four-thousand-year-old conflict) is keeping most of us from really
looking at the facts of the conflict. If we look at it as a sixty-year-old
conflict, rather than a four-thousand-year-old conflict, we can get
a better handle on the real issues of the current conflict. We can
then, with God's help, begin to discover ways to heal it, end it,
and forge a path to peace.

Before I leave this subject (destroying the myth), let me share with you a personal experience that may help you overcome clinging to the myth. Even if you believe the fact (sixty) versus the myth (four thousand), you will revert back to the myth until you fully embrace the fact, and focus on the fact long enough.

I grew up in the South. Does that make me a redneck? Watch out for labels, they'll bite you. Can anybody learn anything from a redneck? Read on.

When I began college in the North, my new northern friends came to realize I was a bigot and very biased. They told me the truth about myself, but I couldn't believe them. It took time for me to realize they were right and I was wrong. The facts of my bigotry were hard to overcome because I grew up believing all I heard. When I came back to the South and started telling my friends what I had learned up North, I lost a lot of friends. It took me years to overcome the wrong I had learned in my childhood, but, thank God, with the help, love, patience, kindness, and understanding of a lot of friends, I was able to overcome a lot of beliefs I had been told were the truth which were not. These horrible myths I had learned in my childhood years were not facts; they were myths.

The narrative of the Middle East conflict is rather simple. It's not too hard to understand. What make it hard are the myths, the misinformation, and the disinformation. At a cursory glance, it is real easy to say, "Oh, it's too complicated." It's not. Please be patient with me as I try to unravel some of the garbage that fills the air and look at the facts.

I remember, in the 1960s, when the south began integrating, that everyone was saying it will never work. The voices of the day were saying it's going to take two hundred years to overcome all this hatred. Look at the progress that has been made in the past fifty years on this issue. All the problems haven't been solved, but look at the progress that has been made. They were wrong. Are we there yet? Of course not, but we've come a long way, and it hasn't been anywhere near two hundred years. The same is true of the Middle East conflict. It can be solved. Peace can be achieved, and it won't take two hundred years.

It is my hope that this book serves as a wake-up call to you. I am asking you to have an open mind and bear with me as I try to make some sense out of this difficult subject. I'm reminded of a hymn we used to sing in church. "Let there be peace on Earth and let it begin with me."

If it's peace in the Israel/Palestine conflict that you want to see happen, then kiss the myth good-bye and wipe the dust off the chalkboard and stand up for what's right and best for both sides, Israel and Palestine.

God's Mandate

God has mandated that I respect the Jews because they are his chosen people. Therefore, as a professing Christian, I must respect the Jew because God loves them and he loves me and he wants me to love them. That is not to say, however, that I must accept every unlawful thing that they do. It doesn't make me anti-Semitic just because I criticize their unlawful behavior or point out the injustices that they commit. However, the moment anyone criticizes them for anything they do; Israel brands them as anti-Semitic. This is not biblical, and it is certainly not true.

Chapter 2

Lead Up to a Crises between Israel and Palestine

In addressing this issue, when did the Palestine/Israeli peace process begin? Where did the term "Middle East peace process" begin? It began when the Soviet Union dismantled.

The person that is responsible for the beginning of this process is Secretary of State James Baker.

When the Soviet Union dismantled, He came up with the brilliant idea that if Russia was no longer an obstacle and was no longer the number one critic against the United States for its involvement in the Middle East, the time was historically right to bring about peace with Palestine/Israel.

James Baker persuaded President Ronald Reagan to initiate what was then labeled as the "Middle East peace process." President Reagan gave him the go-ahead, and Secretary of State James Baker is the unsung hero who started this whole thing. He went to the region eighteen times in order to jump-start the process. He was relentless. He would not give up. He overcame incredible obstacles. In his book, *"The Politics of Diplomacy,"* he spells out what he was up against. He is the *"hero"*—not the unsung hero. We should all be indebted to him. I recommend that everyone reading this will write him a letter and thank him for all that he has done. Secretary of State, James Baker, deserves his place in history. I believe every Secretary of State after James Baker—Christopher Warren, Madeleine Albright, William Powell, Condoleezza Rice, and Hillary Clinton, would all agree with me.

Where to Start?

We don't have to begin with the book of Genesis, but we do have to begin somewhere. An approximate timeframe is "the beginning of modern Israel or approximately 1948." We can certainly use 1948 as a point of reference.

Before we focus on 1948, we need a little background information leading up to the formation of the Israeli state.

We begin with the world Zionist Congress and then explain the significance of the Balfour declaration and sharpen our understanding of how the British mandate figures into the picture.

Of course, the context for the formulation of modern Israel must include what happened just a few short years before 1948, when, during World War II in Europe, Hitler tried to exterminate all European Jews. No one can really comprehend the horror.

Those closest to the Holocaust, the living survivors today, are the ones that are the most sensitive to the issue. We must have empathy and be understanding to the sensitivities of the living survivors.

This horror is a daily reminder to them, and it will take generations for the pain to subside. We must learn to share their pain.

The Holocaust Memorial in Israel, is a grim reminder of this horror and portrays a vivid picture of this tragedy.

When I visited the Holocaust Memorial in Israel, I was so emotionally shaken; I could not stop crying. An Israeli Air Force officer and his wife, who were picnicking at the Memorial, came over to me and gave me aid. I thank God for that man and his wife. They were so sensitive, gentle, and kind.

We spent a good part of the day together, and they explained to me many things that I never would have known were it not for them. They suggested I read the account of the Crusades that occurred over a thousand years ago.

Most of the Crusades was enacted in Israel/Palestine, including the land occupied by Israel today.

Reading about the Crusades provides a keen perspective on the remarkable history of the Holy Land. Every Christian should be knowledgeable of, perhaps, the blackest eye in the history of Christendom.

From Yad Vashem (Holocaust Memorial), one can see Deir Yassin, another sight of a massacre in recent history.

Most visitors to Yad Vashem do not know the story of Deir Yassin, but they should. It tells another story we all should know. The Israelis, of all people, should know it, and yet many do not. In stark contrast, every Palestinian knows the story of Deir Yassin, and they also know the story of Yad Vashem. While Palestinians acknowledge the horror of Yad Vashem, they are not to be blamed for the Holocaust. They took no part in it. They were in Palestine, not Germany. It was the Nazis that did the killing. It was not the Palestinians. And yet many Palestinians today feel that the Israelis are doing to the Palestinians what the Nazis did to the Jews. The Palestinians say, *We are the Jews, We are being killed by the Nazis* (The State of Israel). *We are the victims."*

The Palestinians ask, "*Why has the church in America ignored and abandoned us? Why does America allow Israel to take our homes, to take our land? We have been here for thousands of years. The Israelis do not want us to exist. Is it wrong to call what they're doing to us ethnic cleansing?"*

Look at what Israel is doing today in Gaza. Are they not trying to exterminate nearly two million unarmed civilians in Gaza?

I'm not trying to be an alarmist here, but I hope you will acknowledge that the Palestinians have a legitimate complaint.

After the 1920 Arab riots and 1921 Jaffa riots, the Jewish leadership in Palestine believed that the British, to whom the League of Nations had given a mandate over Palestine in 1920, had no desire to confront local Arab gangs which frequently attacked Palestinian Jews. Believing that they could not rely on the British administration for protection from these gangs, the Jewish leadership created the Haganah to protect Jewish farms and Kibbutzim. In addition to guarding Jewish communities, the role of the Haganah was to warn the residents of and repel attacks by Palestinian Arabs. In the period between 1920-1929, the Haganah lacked a strong central authority or coordination. Haganah "units" were very localized and poorly armed: they consisted mainly of Jewish farmers who took turns guarding their farms or their kibbutzim. Following the 1929 Palestine riots, the Haganah's role changed dramatically. It became a much larger organization, encompassing nearly all the youth and adults in the Jewish settlements, as well as thousands of members from the cities. It also acquired foreign arms and began to develop workshops to create hand grenades and simple military equipment, transforming from an untrained militia to a capable underground army.

In 1936, the Haganah fielded ten thousand mobilized men along with forty thousand reservists. During the 1936-1939 Arab revolt in Palestine, it participated actively to protect British interests and to quell Arab rebellion using the FOSH, and then HISH units. Although the British administration did not officially recognize the Haganah, the British security forces cooperated with it by forming the Jewish Settlement Police, Jewish Auxiliary Forces, and Special Night Squads, which were trained and led by Colonel Orde Wingate. The battle experience gained during this time was to become very useful in the 1948 Arab-Israeli war.

Many Haganah fighters objected to the official policy of havlagah (restraint) that Jewish political leaders (who had become increasingly controlling of the Haganah) had imposed on the militia. Fighters had been instructed to only defend communities and not initiate counterattacks against Arab gangs or their communities.

This policy appeared defeatist to many who believed that the best defense is a good offense and, in 1931, the most militant elements of the Haganah splintered off and formed the Irgun Tsva'i-Leumi (National Military Organization), better known as "Irgun" (or by its Hebrew acronym, pronounced "Etzel"). In 1940, the Irgun also split over the issue of whether or not to attack the British during World War II, and their off-shoot became known as the "Lehi" (Hebrew acronym of Lochamei Herut Yisrael, standing for Fighters for the Freedom of Israel, widely known as the "Stern Gang" after its leader, Abraham Stern).

The significance of Deir Yassin dates back to 1948. At that time, Dier Yassin was a village of approximately 750 peaceful Palestinian residents. The village lay outside of the area set aside by the United Nations for the Jewish State, but its location was of military value because it was located on high ground in the quarter between Tel Aviv and Jerusalem. Early on the morning of Friday, April 9, 1948, several weeks before the end of the British mandate ruling in Palestine, one hundred and thirty commandos from the Stern gang attacked Dier Yassin. By the end of the day, hundreds of Palestinian children, women, and men were killed in the massacre. The Haganah leaders distanced themselves from participation in the attack and issued a statement denouncing the Stern Gang, terrorists units. They admitted that the massacre was a disgrace to the cause of Jewish fighters, and there were a lot of Jewish arms to the Jewish flag. They played down the five that there Paul blocked troops had reinforced in the terrorist attack, even though they did not participate in the massacre and looting subsequent to it.

David Ben-Gurion even sent an apology to King Abdullah, leader of Trans-Jordon. But according to Menachem Begin, the leader of the Irgun, a terrorist organization, at the time, (although he was not at Deir Yassin), "This horrific act assured the future of the state of Israel well." In his book, The Revolt, Menachem Begin claimed: "Arabs throughout the country induced to believe while titles all ergot witchery were seized and limitless panicked and started to flee for their lives. This mass flight soon developed into a maddened, uncontrollable stampede. The political and economic significance of this development can hardly be overestimated."

Of about 144 houses at Deir Yassin, only a few were destroyed. By September, Orthodox Jewish organizations from Poland, Romania, and Slovakia settled there over the objections of Martin Buber, Cecil Roth, and others, who believed that the site of the massacres should be left uninhabited. At the center of the village, the remains of an old cemetery were bulldozed and like hundreds of other problems to villages to follow in Deir Yassin was wiped off the map as the lands of Deir Yassin became a part of the city and is now known simply as the area between the lot show where the settlement of our North.

Deir Yassin, now an organization of Jews and non-Jews, has a mission to make sure that this massacre will never be forgotten. This single event is one of the most significant of the twentieth-century Palestinian and Israeli history, not because of its size or its brutality, but because it marked the beginning of the deportation rule wherein four-hundred Arab villages and cities and the expulsion of over seven-hundred-thousand Palestinian inhabitants took place. my room for the victims of the Holocaust and other Jews from the rest of the world. The story during the same is a story of two people's struggle for the sign land, the details of that story are important for both the victor and the victim.

Although most scholars no longer believe that Israel was a land without people or people without a land, many others believe the myth today, resurrecting the memory of Deir Yassin and serve to dispel this propaganda. Palestinians were dispossessed in 1948 and continue to be dispossessed today in the name of building and expanding a Jewish state.

The significance of Deir Yassin and its ethnic cleansing and the ethnic cleansing of over four hundred villages that followed should be a reminder to the world of the Palestinian Holocaust.

We are taught that there was only one Holocaust, and that refers to the persecution of the Jews by the Nazis. Palestinians are simply not allowed to acknowledge their Holocaust, the persecution of the Palestinians by the Jews. The Jews claim that

Deir Yassin was a "depopulation," a "making room" for a *truly* persecuted people who were returning to the land from which they were driven two thousand years ago. It's like saying our loss was bigger than your loss, so your loss doesn't count.

Enough of the blame game—let's begin to get to the heart of the matter by reviewing more of the true origins of this conflict.

Chapter 3

Journey to the East

Our Christian Holy Land tour arrived in Tel Aviv in mid-1972. Actually, this was not the beginning of the Journey. Perhaps, I should go back a bit and mention what happened prior to our trip to the Holy Land. I believe this will help my readers understand why I went to the Holy Land in the first place.

What started this quest or journey was the California Earthquake of 1971. The epicenter was in Sylmar. It occurred at 6:00 a.m. and lasted sixty-one seconds. That was the longest minute I have ever spent in my entire life. Sixty-five people were killed and two hospitals were leveled to the ground. Freeways were split in half. Had it not occurred so early in the morning, thousands would have lost their lives. To say the least, it was an "earthshaking" experience.

I was in the office, making three hundred copies of a speech I was to deliver to the Inland Empire Homebuilders Association for a 7:00 a.m. breakfast. When I pressed copy; on the copier, it started shaking and jumping all over the room. I looked up and saw the chandeliers swaying back and forth. For the life of me, somehow, I just couldn't seem to comprehend what was happening. The thought of an earthquake never entered my mind.

Our vice president, who was to introduce me at the breakfast, was with me, and he started running for the door out of the building. Not knowing what else to do, I followed him. He ran outside and got on his knees on the lawn and looked up and started crying and saying out loud: "I'm ready Lord, take me home." He thought it was the Rapture. I thought he was losing his mind and becoming far too hysterical. Then, I looked down Citrus Boulevard, and for a straight mile, the street was lined with palm trees, then telephone poles. For a solid mile, they were swaying back and forth as if an underwater ocean was moving and causing them to sway back and forth. It was a sea of movement too awesome to comprehend. I turned 180 degrees to look the other way and what I saw was the most frightening thing I had ever seen in my life. I was looking at the San Gabriel Mountains, and they were moving up and down. What was more freighting was the sound. As one mountain moved up and the other down, the sound was as if the earth was splitting in two. In my fear, I thought it was a nuclear bomb about to explode, but no mushroom cloud. Then, I thought it was an invasion from outer space and a giant space ship was going to come up behind the mountains. The thunderous sound was so powerful that I thought it was the end of the world. The ground immediately under me was moving up and down like a trampoline. Although I was standing on a concrete entrance of the building, it seemed like we were about to be swallowed up into the ground.

"Why I didn't think earthquake?" I'll never know. Maybe because I thought our vice president was flipping out, I thought it was the end times mentioned in the bible.

After the minute and one second, which to me was like an eternity, the noise and rumbling subsided and calm came back.

I called my wife in Westwood, some forty miles inland toward LA to see if she was OK. She said, all the dishes in the cabinets in the kitchen were broken and all the canned goods in the cabinets were on the floor. The house had a crack in it from the front of the house to the back of the house, but more importantly, she and our eight-month-old daughter were OK. Next, I called my stockbroker in Beverly Hills and asked him what he knew. He said rather calmly, "Oh, it was just an earthquake. God just wanted to pull the rug out from under us just to get our attention."

It was then that I began to understand it was an earthquake; but his comment "God" really threw me. I said, "Who are you kidding? I know you, and I know you don't believe in God."

He said, "If you don't believe, I believe in God, then you don't know me at all."

That statement started the beginning of my journey. Is there really a God? It was that experience and that statement that began my quest that led me to the Holy Land.

To be sure, I got closer to God than ever before in my life, and I wanted to go back to the Holy Land to discover more.

Please be patient with me. This is just another piece of the puzzle. When you have finished this book, you will have all the pieces and then you will see the picture. Read on.

Chapter 4

World Zionist Congress

The world Zionist congress was established in 1897. The first Zionist Congress was to have taken place in Munich, Germany. However, due to considerable opposition by the local community leadership, both Orthodox and Reform, it was decided to transfer the proceedings to Basel, Switzerland.

Herzl acted as chairperson of the Congress which was attended by some two hundred participants. The major achievements of the Congress were its formulation of the Zionist platform, known as the Basel program and the foundation of the World Zionist Organization. The program stated,

Zionism seeks for the Jewish people a publicly recognized legally secured homeland.

This gave clear expression to Herzl's political Zionism in contrast with the settlement-orientated activities of the more loosely organized Hibbat Zion. Herzl was elected president of the Zionist organization, and an Inner Actions Committee and a Greater Actions Committee were elected to run the affairs of the movement between Congresses.

In his diary, Herzl wrote,

"Were I to sum up the Basel Congress in a word—which I shall guard against pronouncing publicly—it would be this: At Basel, I founded the Jewish State."

From Herzl's diaries: 3 September 1897:

Everything rested on my shoulders; and this is not just something I am telling myself, for it was proved when on the afternoon of the third day I left because of fatigue and turned the chairmanship over to Nordau. Then everything was helter-skelter, and I was told afterward that it was pandemonium. Even before I took the chair, things did not click.

From Herzl's Opening Address:

We are here to lay the foundation stone of the house which is to shelter the Jewish nation.

In this epoch, in other respects one of such high achievement, we are surrounded by the ancient hatred. Antisemitism is the well-known modern name of the movement.

The modern, educated, de-ghetto-ized Jew, who felt himself stabbed to the heart. Today we can say this calmly, without being suspected of making a play for the tearful compassion of our enemies. Our conscience is clear. The world has always been badly misinformed about us. The feeling of unity among us, which the world so often and so bitterly throws up to us, was in process of dissolution when the tide of antisemitism rose about us. Antisemitism has given us our strength again. We have returned home. Zionism is the return of the Jews to Judaism even before they return to the Jewish land.

We Zionists seek, for the solution of the Jewish question, not an international society, but international discussion . . . We have nothing to do with conspiracy, secret intervention, or indirect models. We wish to put the question in the arena and under the control of free public opinion.

Concerning the colonization efforts in the Argentine (first choice) and in Palestine (third choice). (Actually Austria was choice number two). We shall never speak except in terms of the most genuine gratitude. But these were the opening, and not the closing words of the Zionist movement. This movement must become greater, if it is to be at all. A people can be helped only by itself; and if it cannot do that, then it cannot be helped. We Zionists seek to awaken the Jewish people everywhere to self-help.

The basis can be only that of recognized right, and not of sufferance. We have had our fill of experience with toleration and with the protected Jew. Our movement can be logical and consistent only in so far as it aims at the acquisition of a publicly recognized legal guarantee.

All this my friends and I have repeated over and over again, and we shall not tire of repeating it until we are understood everywhere. On this occasion too, which witnesses the bringing together of Jews from so many scattered lands in response to the ancient call of the nation, we shall repeat it. Must we not feel, hanging over us, the intimidation of great things to come, when we reflect on the hundreds of thousands of Jews whose eyes are now fixed on us in hope and expectation? Within a few hours, the results of our common counsel will be carried out to the ends of the earth. It is therefore our duty to send forth a message of clarification and reassurance. That which the individual says or writes may be passed unnoticed, but not that which issues from this Congress. And finally, it is the duty of this Congress to see to it that when its sessions have come to an end, we do not relapse into our previous condition of disorganization.

We must create here and now and organ, a permanent organ, which the Jewish people has lacked till now. The enterprise is greater than the ambition of willfulness of any individual. If it is to succeed at all, it must rise to a level of high impersonality. And our Congress shall endure far into the future, not only until the day when our need has been met, but far beyond—perhaps then more than ever. Today, we meet on the soil of this friendly nation. Where shall we be a year from now?

Before Max Nordau's address, the Praesidium of the Congress was elected, in accordance with the plan adopted at the preliminary conference. Herzl was president, Nordau First Vice-President.

After Nordau's address came, the reports from the various countries. Nathan Birnbaum and David Farbstein, in supplementary addresses dealt with the sociological and economic aspects of the movement.

The Basel Program

Zionism sought to secure for the Jewish people a publicly recognized, legally secured homeland in Palestine. For the achievement of its purpose, the Congress envisaged the following methods:

1.) The programmatic encouragement of the settlement of Palestine with Jewish agricultural workers, laborers, and artisans.
2.) The unification and organization of all Jewry into local and general groups in accordance with the laws of their respective countries.
3.) The strengthening of Jewish self-awareness and national consciousness.
4.) The preparation of activity for the obtaining of the consent of the various governments, necessary for the fulfillment of the aim of Zionism.

The Creation of an Organization

The second important task was the creation of an organization. Here the difficulty consisted of the possible clash with the laws of the various countries: in many places, membership in international organizations was forbidden by law. The Congress therefore had to content itself with the creation of a general framework; the integration of the various local bodies and the form of membership had to be left to each country.

The Congress was declared to be "the chief organ of the Zionist movement." The basis of electoral right was to be the payment of at least a shekel—which was taken at that time to be the equivalent of one German mark. The Congress was to elect an "Actions Committee"—"Aktionskomitee," with its permanent seat in Vienna. Of its membership, five were to be residents of Vienna, and these were to constitute the actual Executive (Inneres Aktionskomitee); the remainder were to be elected from the various national organizations.

The Instruments of Action

Max Bodenheimer reported on the numerous plans which had been suggested, and proposed the formation of a bank and of a National Fund. Professor Shapira had already proposed a National Fund in "Die Welt," and now he urged the adoption of the plan. Schnirer proposed that no further immigration into Palestine be undertaken before the status of "legal security and public recognition" had been accorded to the aims of the movement; the existing colonies were to be looked upon and supported as "experimental stations." Kaminka reported on the colonization work done till that time. Adam Rosenberg of New York spoke on general conditions in Palestine. Bambus defended the practical work. Heinrich Loewe, part of his address was delivered in Hebrew, announced the agreement of the Palestinians to the plans of the Congress. Marcus Ehrenpreis delivered an address on the Hebrew language, and Prof. Shapira demanded the creation of a Hebrew University in Palestine.

Chapter 5

Balfour Declaration

The Balfour Declaration of 1917 isn't some profound document that was written to astound it's readers with life changing insights. Nor is it known as a "must read" for anyone seeking to find the true meaning of life. It is, however, a document that changed the course of history for the Jewish people. Please indulge me to offer a little background to help the reader understand its significance.

To call the Balfour Declaration of 1917 a document would be a gross overstatement. The entire declaration is one paragraph. The total number of words is only sixty-seven. This is hardly enough to call this profound writing. We need to go back in time just a bit in order to get its significance.

Remember, back in chapter two, "re: the World Zionist Congress?" This is where we can find what led up to the declaration. The Zionists wanted to find a homeland they could call their own. They went all over the world trying to find a place or a country that would permit them to settle there. After much searching, they came up with three choices that they were either offered land or given permission to settle: Australia, Palestine, and Austria.

Australia offered them all the land they wanted if that was where they wanted to settle.

Austria was not opposed because a lot of Jews were already living there. There wasn't a lot of hope for Palestine, because the Jews believed they couldn't get approval from Great Britain.

Enter Lord Balfour. When the Jews pleaded with him, he found favor with their desires and wrote his famous paragraph that changed the destiny of the Jewish people from then until now.

The *"Balfour Declaration of 1917"* (dated 2 November 1917) was a formal statement of policy by the British government stating that

> *His Majesty's government view with favour the establishment in Palestine of a national home for the Jewish people, and will use their best endeavours to facilitate the achievement of this object, it being clearly understood that nothing shall be done which may prejudice the civil and religious rights of existing non-Jewish communities in Palestine, or the rights and political status enjoyed by Jews in any other country.*

This gave Israel the "green like" Israel needed in order to enter Palestine.

Simple enough, so it seemed at the time. Now, let's fast forward to 1948 and take a glimpse of what actually happened. Keep in mind, there were two preconditions to the Declaration: "It being clearly understood that nothing shall be done which may prejudice the *civil* and *religious rights* of existing non-Jewish communities in Palestine."

Chapter 6

British Mandate

The Palestine Mandate, also known as the British Mandate of Palestine or for Palestine was a legal instrument for the administration of Palestine formally approved by the League of Nations in June 1922. It was based on a draft by the principal Allied and associated powers after the First World War. The mandate formalized British rule in Palestine from 1917-1948. The boundaries of two new states were laid down within the territory of the Mandate, Palestine and Transjordan. The preamble of the mandate declared:

Whereas the Principal Allied Powers have also agreed that the Mandatory should be responsible for putting into effect the declaration originally made on November 2, 1917, by the British Government and adopted by the said Powers, in favor of the establishment in Palestine of a national home for the Jewish people; it being clearly understood that nothing should be done which might prejudice the civil and religious rights of existing non-Jewish communities in Palestine or the rights and political status enjoyed by Jews in any other country.

The formal objective of the League of Nations Mandate system was to administer parts of the defunct Ottoman Empire, which had been in control of the Middle East since the sixteenth century, "until such time as they are able to stand alone."

Chapter 7

Al-Haq-B'Tselem

It was a warm afternoon as I was walking down the main street in Ramallah (about 14 miles north of Jerusalem) when I saw a sign outside a building on my right. It read Al-Haq. There was also an arrow pointing up, meaning that the office was upstairs. Not knowing what it was and wanting to satisfy my own curiosity, I walked up the stairs to the third floor and saw "Al-Haq" on the door.

A kind, gentle, young man opened the door, and with a quiet voice, said, "May I help you?"

I said, "I'm a pilgrim from the United States trying to learn about Ramallah. What, I have learned is that my father was the Mukhtar, (The chosen one) and I was wondering what is Al-Haq."

He was very courteous and invited me in. We sat down at an empty table. He offered me a cup of their delicious coffee which I graciously accepted. As we chatted, he started telling me about his organization.

Al-Haq (Law in the service of man) is a human rights organization founded by a group of lawyers from Switzerland. They have trained fieldworkers that interview victims and witnesses of human rights abuses. Al-Haq has put together documents that the witnesses and victims must sign. In the documents, it is stated that they must tell the truth and if it is later found out that they didn't tell the truth that they could be subject to arrest and or imprisonment.

Their goal is to get the word out all over the world about the human rights abuses of Palestinian citizens by the IDF (Israeli Defense forces), more popularly known as the Israeli military, and sanctioned by the Israeli Government.

My first reaction was to comment that this could put both the military and government in a bad light, and why wouldn't the government and or the Israeli military shut them down?

His response was, "Oh, they immediately discredit us as a fanatical group of Palestinians, and nothing we say or do has any legitimate credibility. They don't see us as any kind of threat." Even so, Al-Haq was steadfast and wasn't about to cave in. They are an honest and hardworking group that is working very hard to get the truth out.

My mistake was not asking if they would send me their reports. What followed was a brief history of Al-Haq.

Al-Haq was established in 1979 by a group of Palestinian lawyers following an extended debate over how best to address the lack of human rights protection mechanisms in the Occupied Palestinian Territory (OPT). When it was founded, Al-Haq became one of the first human rights organizations established in the Arab world.

Al-Haq's focus during its first years was largely limited to analyzing the legal status of Israel as an occupying power in the West Bank including East Jerusalem and the Gaza Strip, and the structures imposed by its military and governmental authorities in the OPT. Al-Haq produced some of the first studies applying principles of international humanitarian law to the Israeli occupation. Al-Haq's early studies on topics such as administrative detention and Israel's resort to the British Defense Emergency Regulations were essential in shaping the debate on what laws and regulations are applicable in the OPT. During this period,

Al-Haq established its legal unit, which together with the legal research unit developed Al-Haq's positions and legal arguments.

By 1986, Al-Haq began taking on special projects regarding human rights issues of particular concern, such as womens' and labor rights. During this time, Al-Haq's work and contributions in the field of human rights began to gain international recognition.

When the first intifada (uprising) broke out toward the end of 1987, Al-Haq again began expanding its work to meet the challenge of addressing violations occurring as a result of this uprising. Although Al-Haq established its fieldwork department in 1983 and the information gathered by its fieldworkers became the backbone of its work, it wasn't until the first intifada erupted, and the resultant demands for information by concerned human rights organizations and activists, media, and others at the national and international level, that the fieldwork department grew to include staff throughout the OPT; consequently, the first intifada proved to be a peak period for Al-Haq's work, activities, and accomplishments.

A number of important Al-Haq campaigns were started during this time and Al-Haq continued to grow, expanding to cover the situation in the Gaza Strip. By the early 1990s, Al-Haq had approximately forty members on staff. Al-Haq's size and its increased professional and human resource capacity helped it to successfully raise awareness of human rights abuses in the OPT and Al-Haq gained international recognition.

The signing of the Oslo Accords in 1993 ushered in a new period in the Israeli-Palestinian conflict. The changes in the political situation that had resulted in the establishment of the Palestinian National Authority (PNA) required that Al-Haq reassess its mission. Despite internal disagreement over how to approach the new situation created by Oslo, Al-Haq began to move forward in work with the PNA, and began, amongst other activities, to monitor the first Palestinian Legislative Council (PLC) elections held in 1996; analyze legislation to ensure that it incorporated human rights standards; and to provide training to PNA law enforcement officials on fundamental human rights principles.

However, some disputes were never resolved, and came to head during late 1996 and early 1997, requiring Al-Haq's board to intervene and terminate all staff contracts, thereby leaving the future of the organization in doubt.

In 1998, Al-Haq began to rebuild. Al-Haq's board of directors hired new staff and took over many of the organization's administrative responsibilities. The organization's focus was also changed with the board taking the decision that Al-Haq should focus on legal research and little attention on monitoring and documentation activities. Work following up on drafting PLC legislation and Israeli human rights violations moved forward.

Toward the end of 1999, Al-Haq was granted special consultative status with the UN Economic and Social Council, thereby enabling it to work once more at the international level, and at the UN level in particular. Financially stable and with its departments rebuilt, by the time the second intifada began in September 2000, Al-Haq was prepared to face the challenges that this uprising brought and the increased Israeli violations in response to it.

In 2002, Israeli occupying forces stepped up the violations of the rights of the Palestinian civilian population by carrying out large scale military incursions into much of the West Bank, including Ramallah. During these incursions, Israel targeted the social, economic, and political infrastructure of the PNA and raided and destroyed hundreds of governmental and non-governmental offices. On March 31, 2002, Israeli forces broke into Al-Haq's office and destroyed much of its equipment.

From 2002 onwards, Al-Haq continued to focus its efforts on restructuring its programmatic, financial, and administrative systems, and undertook an extensive revision of its fundamental goals and objectives, and how its various activities relate to the organization's vision and mandate. In addition, Al-Haq became increasingly active on lobbying the PLC to include human rights standards in Palestinian legislation and spearheaded activities by human rights organizations and other civil society organizations to ensure their active participation in the process for the passage of key legislation on issues of concern, and strengthen their capacity to do so.

By the beginning of 2004, the organization completed the process of adjusting its legal status and was able to register as a non-governmental organization under the Palestinian NGO law (No. 1 for the year 2000).

In 2004, coinciding with the twenty-fifth anniversary of the establishment of Al-Haq, the organization launched a campaign against Israeli measures of collective punishment and intimidation in the OPT. In addition to the campaign, Al-Haq marked its twenty-fifth anniversary with "Waiting for Justice," a report that provided in-depth legal analysis of violations of human rights by the Israeli authorities, based on firsthand information gathered by its fieldworkers.

In August 2005, Al-Haq commissioned an in-depth external evaluation of its organizational structure and policies to identify overall strengths, weaknesses, and major challenges facing Al-Haq, and to assess the relevance and quality of its various programs and activities.

Other than considering the organization's administrative and financial structure, the final evaluation report drew up recommendations for Al-Haq's future development to improve its effective operation at the programmatic and structural levels and ensure its institutional sustainability. This evaluation facilitated and fed recommendations into the development of a subsequent five-year strategic plan (2006-2010) in September 2005, concerning the future direction of Al-Haq's mandate and work.

Al-Haq's Milestones.

1979 Al-Haq: Law in the Service of Man is established, and becomes an affiliate of the International Commission of Jurists based in Geneva.
1983 Al-Haq's first fieldworker is hired.
1986 Legal research focus expands: seminal papers on the issues of administrative detention and the British Defense

Regulations are produced, stimulating debate at the local and international levels regarding Israeli policies in the OPT.

1987 The first intifada erupts. Al-Haq expands staff to meet the challenge of addressing increased violations arising from Israeli policies to quell the intifada.

1988

- Al-Haq hosts an international conference on the administration of the OPT.
- The "Enforcement Project," focusing on calling upon the international community to uphold international law, is launched.
- Al-Haq publishes its first annual report.
- Al-Haq's lawyers establish the right of Palestinian representatives to be present at autopsies performed on people killed by Israeli occupying forces in unclear circumstances.
- Five of Al-Haq's fieldworkers are administratively detained.

1989

- An external evaluation of Al-Haq's structure is carried out. Discussions begin regarding administrative, financial, and managerial policies and structures.
- Al-Haq's general director resigns. Internal debates and conflicts begin over the successor.
- Al-Haq receives the Carter-Menil Human Rights Prize.

1990 Al-Haq's monitoring and documentation efforts results in opening up new Israeli investigation into the events of the Al-Aqsa massacre.

1991 Al-Haq launches its family unification campaign.

1996 Al-Haq monitors the first Palestinian legislative elections to take place following the signing of the Oslo Accords and the establishment of the PNA.

1997   Internal conflicts at Al-Haq snowball, causing the board of directors to terminate the contracts of its entire staff.

1998

- The board changes from being a policy-oriented one to an administrative one. Internal structures and mechanisms are frozen.
- A new staff plus one of the previous staff members are hired by Al-Haq, and focus is placed on legal research.
- Al-Haq's fieldwork and database activities are frozen.
- The organization moves from project to core funding.
- Work on developing Palestinian legislation and influencing the PLC becomes a major area of focus.

1999

- Al-Haq continues to work on a project basis.
- Emphasis is placed on increasing funds channeled to Al-Haq and diversifying funding sources. Several long-term donor organizations renew their relationships with Al-Haq.
- Al-Haq's fieldwork and database activities remain frozen.
- Al-Haq is the first Palestinian human rights organization to be granted special consultative status with the UN Economic and Social Council.

2000

- Al-Haq's Monitoring and Documentation Unit is revived.
- The second intifada breaks out.

2001

- Al-Haq's general director resigns in August, and a new one is appointed before the end of the year.
- Renewed emphasis is placed on Al-Haq's traditional areas of strength: legal research, fieldwork, and documentation.

- Al-Haq's Monitoring and Documentation Unit becomes fully operational and its activities serve as Al-Haq's backbone.
- Work at the beginning of the year is carried out on an ad-hoc basis in response to Israeli violations in the face of the intifada.
- The new general director begins a process of program planning. Emphasis is put on integrating Al-Haq's various departments and strengthening cooperation and information sharing between them.

2002

- The intifada continues and Israeli human rights violations increase in scale and intensity with Israel's incursions into PNA-controlled Palestinian areas.
- Israeli incursions require the development of an emergency plan.
- Al-Haq begins to move away from working on a project basis to working on a core program basis.
- Al-Haq's board resumes its function as a policy board.

2003 Al-Haq holds the first conference on Palestinian legislation, entitled, "Toward the Establishment of a Palestinian Legislative Strategy."

2004

- Al-Haq celebrates its twenty-fifth anniversary and issues its 2004 annual report "Waiting for Justice."
- The organization launches its campaign against collective punishment from Ramallah and at the World Social Forum in Mumbai, India.
- Al-Haq registers as a non-governmental society under the Palestinian NGO Law No. 1 for the year 2000.

- The organization elects nine new members to the board of directors for the next three years, as well as twenty-eight members to the general assembly.

2005

- Al-Haq jointly participates in monitoring the Palestinian presidential elections with international observers from the International Commission of Jurists, and publishes its main observations in a separate report.
- Al-Haq commissions an in-depth external evaluation of its organizational structure and policies to identify overall strengths, weaknesses, and major challenges facing Al-Haq, and to asses the relevance and quality of its various programs and activities. External evaluators publish a joint evaluation report highlighting their main conclusions and recommendations.
- The organization begins a process of strategic planning that culminates in Al-Haq's next five-year strategic plan.
- Al-Haq's fieldworker in the Bethlehem area is administratively detained.
- The organization convenes an expert seminar titled "From Theory to Practice: Upholding International Humanitarian Law in the Occupied Palestinian Territories" on November 1.

B'Tselem

In or about 1987, a member of the Israeli Kennesitt learned about Al-Haq and their hard work and struggles and decided to form an Israeli human rights watch chronicling the human rights abuse handed down on the Palestinians. His reasoning was Israel wouldn't discredit them if the information came from a legitimate Israeli organization. He was right. They gained credibility right from the start. B'Tselem solicited the help of Al-Haq to equip them with the proper way to get things started the right way. B'Tselem attested that it was because of the help of Al-Haq that B'Tselem started getting noticed from the get go.

What follows is a brief history of B'Tselem.

B'Tselem—The Israeli Information Center for Human Rights in the Occupied Territories was established in 1989 by a group of prominent academics, attorneys, journalists, and Knesset members. It endeavored to document and educate the Israeli public and policymakers about human rights violations in the Occupied Territories, combat the phenomenon of denial prevalent among the Israeli public, and help create a human rights culture in Israel.

B'Tselem in Hebrew literally means "in the image of," and is also used as a synonym for human dignity. The word is taken from Genesis 1:27 "And God created man in his image. In the image of God did He create him." It is in this spirit that the first article of the Universal Declaration of Human Rights states that "All human beings are born equal in dignity and rights."

As an Israeli human rights organization, B'Tselem acts primarily to change Israeli policy in the Occupied Territories and ensure that its government, which rules the Occupied Territories, protects the human rights of residents there and complies with its obligations under international law.

B'Tselem is independent and is funded by contributions from foundations in Europe and North America that support human rights activity worldwide and by private individuals in Israel and abroad.

B'Tselem has attained a prominent place among human rights organizations. In December 1989, along with Al-Haq B'Tselem received the Carter-Menil Award for Human Rights at the President Jimmy Carter presidential center in Atlanta, Georgia. The prize included a $500,000 cash award. B'Tselem's reports have gained B'Tselem a reputation for accuracy, and the Israeli authorities relate to them seriously. B'Tselem ensures the reliability of information it publishes by conducting its own fieldwork and research, the results of which are thoroughly cross-checked with relevant documents, official government sources, and information from other sources, among them, Israeli, Palestinian, Al-Haq, and other human rights organizations.

Activities

The focus on documentation reflects B'Tselem's objective of providing as much information as possible to the Israeli public, since information is indispensable to taking action and making choices. Readers of B'Tselem publications may decide to do nothing, but they cannot say, "We didn't know."

Reports

B'Tselem has published scores of reports, some comprehensive in scope, covering most kinds of human rights violations that have occurred in the Occupied Territories. The reports have dealt, for example, with torture, fatal shootings by security forces, restriction on movement, expropriation of land and discrimination in planning and building in East Jerusalem, administrative detention, and settler violence.

Press conferences are often held when a new report is published. In addition, reports often lead to B'Tselem accompanying and assisting journalists reporting on human rights violations, and to other activities intended to affect public opinion in Israel. What follows are various reports from 1989 to present.

Activity in the Knesset

B'Tselem regularly provides Knesset members with information on human rights violations in the Occupied Territories, and injustices caused by Israeli authorities. Several Knesset members, from various factions, assist B'Tselem in placing human rights matters on the public agenda and in safeguarding human rights.

Public action

B'Tselem has hundreds of supporters and volunteers who work to improve the human rights situation in the Occupied Territories. These activities include, in part, setting up information stands, distributing printed material, addressing problems and requests to decision-makers, and participating in protests in the Occupied Territories.

B'Tselem's contact information
8 HaTa'asiya St. (4th Floor), Jerusalem, Israel.
Mailing address: PO Box 53132, Jerusalem 91531, Israel
Tel: 972-2-6735599, Fax: 972-2-6749111
E-Mail: mail@btselem.org

Questions and answers

Since its founding, certain questions have repeatedly been asked about the organization, among them:

What does B'Tselem do?

B'Tselem promotes respect for human rights in Israel and the Occupied Territories through a variety of means. The document both specific incidents and systemic problems impacting human rights. We maintain an extensive communication with Israeli authorities to ensure that individual cases are addressed, and to encourage a rethinking of policies that are out of step with Israel's legal obligations. The conduct first-class research analyzing the full spectrum of human rights concerns. And we use creative public education and advocacy strategies—including pioneering video advocacy—to generate public discussion and foster positive change.

Why is B'Tselem bringing this work to the United States instead of keeping it in Israel?

American foreign policy plays a vital role in shaping Israel's policies in the Occupied Territories. The debate in the United States is often based on a false dichotomy between Israel's legitimate security concerns on the one hand, and Palestinians' basic rights on the other. As an Israeli human rights group, B'Tselem is uniquely positioned to inform and enrich this debate, providing the facts necessary to evaluate Israeli policy in light of security needs and applicable legal standards. B'Tselem has established a presence in the United States to enable Americans to support a human rights agenda that will protect the rights of Israelis and Palestinians alike, while also strengthening Israel's civil society and its democracy.

Just as B'Tselem's work spurs vigorous debate in Israel about the implications of our control over the West Bank and Gaza Strip, so too does B'Tselem aspire to serve as a resource to promote the same healthy debate within the United States. B'Tselem works in the United States to provide accurate, reliable information to policy makers, opinion shapers, and the public alike about the reality on the ground. Our work is guided by the belief that accurate information is indispensable to effective policy making and broadens and informs the public debate that drives it.

Don't you worry that you are making Israel look bad?

B'Tselem's primary goal is to ensure that Israel respects human rights in the Occupied Territories and fulfills its obligations under international law. Publicity has often proven effective in improving Israeli policies and for this reason we are obligated to publicize policies that harm human rights and run counter to Israel's legal obligations. While B'Tselem reports on some of the least attractive aspects of Israeli policy, in doing so we highlight some of the best aspects of Israeli society. B'Tselem is part of Israel's vibrant, civil society, working in spite of the difficult security situation to improve our society from within. We are proud to represent this part of Israel to a world which is all too often unaware of it.

What does the word "B'Tselem" mean?

B'Tselem's work is rooted both in the Jewish tradition and in the universal principles of international law. Its name in Hebrew literally means "in the image of" and is also used as a synonym for human dignity. The word is taken from Genesis 1:27 "And God created human beings in his image. In the image of God did He create them." This spirit is echoed in the first article of the Universal Declaration of Human Rights: "All human beings are born equal in dignity and rights."

Does B'Tselem report on all human rights violations in the Occupied Territories, or just those committed by Israelis?

B'Tselem sees international law and human rights norms as universal standards that are equally applicable. All Israelis and Palestinians have equal rights to live in dignity and safety, and Israeli and Palestinian authorities must respect these rights. B'Tselem monitors and reports on severe violations of human rights by the Palestinian Authority against their own population, as well as on terror attacks against Israelis. Ultimately, though, B'Tselem is an Israeli organization and our primary concern is the actions of the Israeli government and security forces.

How is B'Tselem's work received by the Israeli government and security forces?

B'Tselem maintains an extensive and multi-faceted relationship with the Israeli authorities. Every year we send hundreds of individual cases to the relevant authorities asking them to investigate allegations of wrongdoing. In turn, these authorities request B'Tselem's assistance in conducting investigations, and B'Tselem locates Palestinian witnesses, encourages them to cooperate with Israeli authorities, and provides other forms of assistance to promote justice and redress.

On the policy-level as well, the Israeli government and military authorities have learned to take B'Tselem's work seriously. Both military and government officials understand that B'Tselem's reports must be addressed in a substantive manner, even if they are unhappy about the content of those reports.

The Israel Defense Forces and other relevant authorities frequently issue formal responses to B'Tselem reports, and these responses are published together with the reports. B'Tselem is also invited to participate in Knesset hearings and meets regularly with military and government officials to voice our concerns. B'Tselem has worked successfully on both the political and public level to shape Israel's national debate over policies regarding the Occupied Territories, and to change Israeli policy to better accord with human rights obligations.

Regarding such a politically polarizing issue as the Israeli-Palestinian conflict, much of the information that comes out of the region is weighted to favor one side or the other. Why should I trust B'Tselem's information?

B'Tselem ensures the reliability of its information through independent fieldwork and rigorous research, the results of which are thoroughly cross-checked with relevant documents, official government sources, and information from other sources, among them Israeli, Palestinian, and other human rights organizations. B'Tselem includes responses from the relevant authorities in its reports whenever we get them, so you can evaluate both our findings and those of the government and make your own judgment.

Why don't you work to protect human rights within Israel?

B'Tselem's energies are intentionally focused exclusively on violations of human rights within the Occupied Territories, where there is a systematic lack of accountability for ensuring the rule of law that endangers the well-being of the population there and undermines Israel's image as a country guided by the rule of law.

A broad spectrum of other Israeli organizations engage in the important work of addressing human rights issues within Israel.

Where does B'Tselem stand on a two-state solution?

B'Tselem's primary goal is to promote Israel's adherence to human rights and international humanitarian law as it applies to Israel's conduct in the Occupied Territories. We support all policies that would substantially decrease or end the violations of human rights under the Occupation. We do not weigh in on political matters, except to comment on their implications for human rights.

Who funds B'Tselem?

B'Tselem is independent and is funded by contributions from foundations in Europe and North America that support human rights activity worldwide, and by foreign governments, and private individuals in Israel and abroad.

What follows are various reports.

> October 1, 1989
> Banned books and authors
> May God preserve the scrolls.

This information sheet details how over twenty thousand books were banned from the West Bank and Gaza. The censor, who cannot be named, mentioned the difficulty in selecting which books were to be chosen. Poetry was completely banned.

Many readers of B'Tselem are not used to smiling. Most of what they read has to do with slaughter and killing. The banning of books has adverse effects on people. It tears out a heart. It causes lasting pain.

Devotion to a book or distancing one's self from a book, precisely because one must accept or oppose a seriously written book; when the book is banned, this choice is lost in the universe of people who read.

Jerusalem, November 1989: "The military judicial system in the West Bank," this 87-page report documents how the military judicial system denies basic rights to Palestinian suspects and detainees.

Jerusalem, February 1990: "The system of taxation in the West Bank and the Gaza Strip," as an instrument for the enforcement of authority during the uprising.

Information sheet, update February-March 1990. "Censorship of the Palestinian Press, in East Jerusalem." This 44-page report shows the unjustifiable infringement upon public and individual freedoms.

Information sheet update April 1990. "Reports on the number of fatalities of Palestinians by the Israeli security forces in the first three months of the year."

It seems in their first year of operation, B'Tselem was ignored by the Israeli Security Forces. However, as time went by, B'Tselem began to gain support by the Israeli public and the security forces began to respect what they were doing.

Jerusalem, July 1990: "The use of firearms by the security forces in the Occupied Territories." This report sets out to examine the substance and the character of the rules of engagement and the changes that have been implemented in the policy regarding the opening of fire during the intifada (uprising). This issue was so important that it was brought to the High Court of Justice. Judicially, the West Bank and Gaza Strip are classified as territories held under belligerent occupation. This level of classification entitled certain rules of behavior and limitations on the inhabitants' right to the protection of their safety and their lives. The level of activities of military force in the territories may not be and indeed is not equivalent to the situation on the battlefield.

Chapter 8

El Hakawadi

El Hakawadi is a Palestinian Thespian Troupe in Jerusalem. They were booked to perform in New York City. While they were en route, a group of anti-Palestinian Jews from New York put so much pressure on the agency that had booked them, threatening the booking agency that they would never patronize the agency again if they allowed the performance. Under threat, the agency canceled.

When El Hakawadi arrived in New York, they were shocked to learn they had been canceled. Not having enough funds to travel back to Palestine and little funds to pay for hotel rooms and food, they called us, the Atlanta chapter of the Palestine Humanitarian Rights Committee (PHRC). As a member of the committee, I was asked to assist.

PHRC called together a meeting to discuss the possibility of having El Hakawadi come to Atlanta to perform, and hopefully, raise enough funds to house them and pay for air travel for their return home back to Palestine. It was not an easy task, but we felt they were in a difficult situation, and it seemed, we were their best hope.

Not knowing exactly what to do or where to start, we contacted the Georgia Screen Actors Guild for their help. We were grateful and they accepted. Without their help, we probably would not have succeeded.

We formed task groups. One group was assigned the task of raising funds for airfare from New York to Atlanta. Another group was tasked to find adequate housing, another for finding a venue and dates of performances. Another was tasked to contact the Atlanta Journal for news coverage and advertisement, another for ticket sales, etc.

It was exciting to see it all come together, but it was not without its challenges.

The Georgia Screen Actors Guild was successful in getting the Alliance Theatre to provide the venue for the performance. This was not without some serious obstacles.

The Atlanta Jewish Council protested and threatened the Alliance Theatre management. They said if the Alliance Theatre allowed the performance to be held, they would never have any Jewish Actors perform at the Alliance theatre. They threatened to have the Alliance Theatre shut down. This is simply another example of their intimidating and threatening tactics. They have pockets and clusters like this all over the United States and they get their way through threats and intimidation. Please don't miss my point. I am not issuing a complaint, I am trying to get the reader to understand their agenda. Remember earlier I pointed out that since 1948 their agenda has been Israeli supremacy and to smear the Palestinian. They continue to do that to this day.

Management of the Alliance Theatre crumbled under the threats and informed us they were canceling the engagement.

The president of the Georgia Screen Actors Guild decided to fight fire with fire and informed the Atlanta Jewish Council if they wanted to threaten to not have any Jewish Actors ever perform at Alliance Theatre, then they would not be allowed to join the Georgia Screen Actors Guild. The Atlanta Jewish Council backed off, and Alliance Theatre rescinded their cancellation and agreed to allow the performance to take place.

The conflict was actually a blessing in disguise because it caused a lot of attention, and everybody wanted to see the performance and see what the fuss was all about.

The performances were held on a weekend two nights in a row. It was a complete sellout.

The play was about a young Palestinian boy living in Palestine who could not take the oppression and intimidation that the Israelis are putting on him,so he moved to America. He enrolled in college, he started his own business, became very successful, but he missed home. A few years later some of his friends came to America to visit him. He was shocked to hear their report. They reported that since he left, Israel had bulldozed thousands of their homes and pushed out the Palestinians and took over four hundred villages. He couldn't believe it. He went back to Palestine and was shocked to see that it was true.

This was a powerful play and it moved the audience to tears. It is almost impossible to imagine that it could be done.

This is a true story. Israel destroyed 400 villages and displaced all of its inhabitants.

Chapter 9

Lifting the Siege of Beit Sahour

One night, I received a call from a local pastor friend in Atlanta. (I will not use his name for fear of Israeli terrorists' reprisals.) There was a very serious incident going on in Israel, and he was asked to go over there to help, but couldn't because of a previous commitment. He was calling me to ask if I could take his place and go to Israel immediately. He briefly described the problem and its urgency.

Almost everyone in America is familiar with the story of the "Boston Tea Party," basically taxation without representation. The incident took place in a small village about two miles east of Bethlehem called Beit Sahour. The citizens were facing a situation that could be described as "taxation without representation."

The predominantly Christian-Palestinian village of Beit Sahour is also known as "Guardian of the Shepherd's Field." It is mentioned at Christmas time in most churches around the world when telling the story about the birth of the baby Jesus: "And the Shepherds were in their fields, watching their flocks by night." From this little valley, the shepherds could look up and see Bethlehem and the star pointing to the manger. No one would ever imagine that two thousand years later, the citizens of Beit Sahour would be facing threats of their very existence by "Modern" Israel.

The people of Beit Sahour were denied any say in how their tax money was used, and they did not receive adequate municipal services in return for their taxes. The taxes were supposed to be used to provide books for school children and fill huge potholes on the streets, among other things. Israel did not provide books for the schools or repair any of the streets, or as it seemed, anything else with the tax proceeds from the people of Beit Sahour, so the citizens decided to take a stand and not to pay the taxes. A tax revolt if, you will.

In response to their defiant stand, the Israeli army sealed off the village; blocked off all the main roads in and out of the village and waged an all-out tax war against the citizens. They invaded the people's homes; confiscating their personal property, in fact confiscating whatever they could lay their hands on, even children's toys.

During these raids, residents of Beit Sahour, especially women and children, had been brutally assaulted by Israeli soldiers and "tax men." Hundreds of its young men were imprisoned without charge or trial, and three—Edmond Ghanem, Yad Bishara, Abu Atallah uslah—were killed. The siege lasted for over forty days.

By this time, parts of the World community were beginning to hear of this and some attempted to investigate. Six emissaries were sent, I believe from Switzerland to Israel to see what was happening and the authorities at the airport would not allow them to go in saying Israel was a sovereign nation and did not need outside help. So they were immediately sent back home and were not allowed outside Tel Aviv.

One of the most respected families in Jerusalem for hundreds of years is the Housani family and the great-grandson, Fisal Housani, regarded as a nonviolent Christian peacemaker, felt he had enough influence to go there and talk to them and find out what had to be done to get the siege lifted. The IDF would not permit him to be admitted and order him to go away.

There were reports coming out of Beit Sahour of Israeli soldiers going inside the village and removing all the medications from the pharmacies taking them outside and destroying them, going into groceries and removing the coolers so that people could not get food, and there were rumors of people starving to death.

Nobody knew how to handle the situation, and the idea was to, as quickly as possible, gather 125 Americans and go over there collectively and march down the street from Bethlehem to Beit Sahour where the barricade was.

I asked what was the downside or risk in this, and was told the worst case scenario would be that we could be shot; a lesser one would be that we would be arrested. But it was believed that the Israelis wouldn't shoot or arrest 125 Americans, and I decided to sleep on it and give my decision whether to go the next day.

I agonized during the night and discussed it in great detail with my wife. I had never done anything like this before and was apprehensive and fearful. I had been involved in many Christian incidences there and really had to do my own soul searching as to say, "Am I going to be a well-wisher on the side? Or am I going to do something if I am asked to help?" The next day I felt I would like to be part of the group, and so I agreed.

I boarded a plane from Atlanta to Dulles Airport and noticed a group of about forty to sixty people gathered together talking. As I approached, I heard them discussing issues in the Middle East. I introduced myself, and it became clear that they were part of the group that was going to Israel, so we boarded a plane to Tel Aviv. I am not sure of the exact composition of the group, but there were doctors, journalists, Vietnam veterans, and experienced activists.

Arrangements had been made for us to stay at the National Hotel in downtown Jerusalem. We arrived at the hotel at about ten thirty at night rather exhausted. We got the keys to our rooms and agreed to have a meeting the next day to develop a strategy on what and how we would go about doing this.

Mr. Landrum Bolling, veteran peacemaker is the President Emeritus of Earlham College and former director of the Tantoric Institute in the Middle East. He has been a peacemaker for many years and in fact has won the National Peace Foundation Award. He is also an advisor to Mercy Corp. He told us we had to get out of the hotel as it was covered with Israeli Undercover Police (Shen bet and Massad) and wouldn't be surprised if every phone in the hotel was tapped, they knew we were there.

We all took our luggage and got on the buses and drove to Bethlehem, but there wasn't a hotel big enough to hold us all, so we divided and stayed in two hotels. The next day was devoted to finding a meeting place where we could all congregate and discuss what we were going to do and how we were going to do it. We found a conference room that was big enough for all of us to have a meeting.

Although the main entrance to Beit Sahour was blocked, there were side roads where one or two people could get out. So we had the mayor of the city and a couple of leaders talk to us about some of the incidents. There were several of us that were able to get into the city and talk to some of the people to get some firsthand knowledge on some of the things that had happened.

I talked to one of the pharmacists who said that they, the soldiers, had come in and taken everything off the shelves, took it outside, and crushed them. I went into the home of a family of a man who was eighty years old and was told that they were traumatized that they could not get medicines for him. There was a woman who said that the soldiers tore into her house and went into her bedroom and took all of her jewelry, and they didn't care who or how they harmed, and treated the people very unmercifully.

We reported back to the group, and I was chosen to go to the American Consulate to explain why we were there and what we were trying to do and get instructions on what we could and could not do. I told them we were a nonviolent group, and we were trying to get the siege lifted and the city opened up, so the people could get food, and we could try to open up dialogue and solve this problem. I also told them that all the people I talked to were happy to pay taxes if they could get something for it, but they were getting nothing.

One of the things occurred whilst we were at the hotel was a gentleman who was in so much despair that he was just looking for help from anybody and wanted to know what he could do to help. We asked him why he was in despair, and he explained that his daughter had recently gone to a funeral and was murdered there, shot by sniper fire. A group of half a dozen of the people we were with said that what they would like to do was get a tree and go to his house and plant it as a memorial to his daughter. He replied that he would like that very much, but he feared that the Israelis would find out about it and do harm to him. But we felt that no harm would come to him as we had CNN reporters there and had a conference after that, and CNN Jerusalem agreed to film it, and it should be put on, we hoped, CNN national. He was reluctant, but said, if we would do this, it would be a good thing to do.

The next morning he came and the Israelis had already found out about it through their own methods, and they had beat this man to the point that he begged for us not to plant the tree as he felt more harm would come to his family.

There was a refugee camp very close to Bethlehem between there and Jerusalem where a group of women went and reported that conditions there were so horrible that it was unbelievable and it was like a prison. It is difficult for me to comprehend where there would be a refugee camp there in the first place.

After a lot of discussions and questions and answers, there some people that were upset that they actually even panicked saying that they were not sure they wanted to go through with this that it was too dangerous. But we finally calm them down and got to know each other better and agreed, I think this was on a Friday night, we planned we would all meet at 7:00 a.m. at a major square in Bethlehem and file about four across and about twenty-five deep and march from Bethlehem to the entrance of Beit Sahour and the Israelis already knew about it and.

Just before we got into Bethlehem, to the right, there was a huge empty lot that had about four-hundred soldiers with tents that they were sitting ready in preparation for whatever may or may not happen. They did not know what our agenda was fully, but they knew we were there, and they knew that something was going to happen.

When we gathered on the Sunday morning to be prepared to walk four wide across, a huge troop carrier with a menacing sound pulled up beside us revving their motor to make us aware that they were there. The vehicle then passed in front of us and slowing down, forcing us to walk at their pace. Another vehicle came along side and one came up on our rear, and it appeared that they were demonstrating that they were in control, escorting us to Beit Sahour, and that they were well prepared for any incident that may occur.

We started singing the song of Martin Luther King Jr. "We Shall Overcome," and we successfully got to enter Beit Sahour where there was a line of about fifty soldiers wide, with another fifty behind then, and a further fifty behind them. So in total, there were around 150 soldiers standing there with arms. Out to the left of this was a jeep. The driver has two stars on each shoulder (perhaps a general). In the passenger seat was a man wearing a sweater with what looked like a goatee beard, and I think he was there as an observer.

When we got up to the front, we saw one of the young, highly polished-looking, proud Israeli soldiers wearing a beautiful burgundy bandetta and carrying an uzzi that had a shoulder strap that was all hand embroidered. It looked like it was prepared for him specially, as if he was a highly regarded hero figure. He seemed to be very gentlemanly and confident and said something like, "Yes, can I help you, please?"

I was on the front row of the march with the mayor of the city and a member of the Chicago Human Rights Campaign. One of the three of us said, "We are from the United States of America, it is Sunday morning, and we would like to go into Beit Sahour and go to church and pray and worship. Do you have a problem with that?"

He said, "One moment please."

The soldier took very guarded formal military back steps and made an about turn, then marched over to the jeep, and had a conversation with the officer. When he returned, his first question was, "Do you have any reporters with you?"

I replied that we had six, and the soldier told us that they would have to stay behind, but the rest of us could go in. So we started marching inside the city of Beit Sahour, and it appeared to be an abandoned village—there was no one in sight. As we continued to walk, we looked up at the windows and could see curtains move as if there was someone behind those curtains looking to see who we were.

Within about five minutes of us entering the city, children came running toward us, with glee as if they were being rescued and they were all shouting "PLO Israel Go!"

The 125 of us soon became around 250, then more people started running, and we grew to about 350. We approached the first church, which was not the one we were going to but one of the outer churches. The pastor of the church stopped the congregation that he was speaking to and asked what this, our march, was all about. We told him, and he went into the church and told everyone there to come with him. The entire church then came to follow us, we swelled up to about a thousand, and by then, the word had seemed to have spread very quickly, and we swelled up to around 1,500 people.

The military officer that was escorting us was beginning to get a little nervous and started shouting back very loudly, "Please let's keep this in order, let's do what you were going to do."

There was one man with our group, who happened to be a pastor but a huge man of about 6 feet 5 inches. He was rather authoritative, was not trying to make trouble, but trying to tell the military officer to back off and not order us around.

We finally arrived at this beautiful church and started marching in, but everybody at the church did not know what to expect. The first thing I noticed was a domed chapel, which had painted on it a picture of Christ holding what appeared to be tablets of Moses or an open book and giving the victory or peace sign. It was a precious moment.

I was just going to sit at the front, but I was pointed over to a family. It was called the Daud family whose son had been in Atlanta and had been found dead a couple of years earlier.

Gratefully we were able to have the siege lifted. This is simply another example of the agenda of Israel to show their supremacy and to make life miserable and unbearable for the Palestinians.

We had two CNN journalists with us. They brought in the Jerusalem CNN journalist who videotaped our conference after the event. Israel was clever enough to have that video confiscated and our report never appeared in the United States television media or newspapers. I reported this incidence to then Senator Sam Nunn of Georgia. We met in Washington DC, in Senator Nunn's office and I had with me the President of the American Vietnam Veterans Association as a witness to the event to corroborate my story because he was with our group in Beit Sahour and he saw everything.

We went to Washington DC and reported this entire incident to Senator Sam Nunn. He assured us he would bring this to the attention of the proper authorities

Chapter 10

Sabeel

In 1972, I attended a Church Service At St. Georges' Anglican Church on Suelman Rd. just outside the Damascas Gate of the Walled City of Jerusalem. The service was performed by the Reverend Dr.Canon Naim Ateek of the Anglican Church.

Some time later, we fortuitously met at the checkpoint border of Israel and Egypt. After we got through the checkpoint, we boarded the bus and sat together all the way to Egypt.

Naim talked at length about a book he was writing and hoped to complete soon. I encouraged him to complete the book and requested a copy on my next trip to Israel.

A few years later the book was published. "Justice only Justice" tells of the struggles of a banker (Naims' father) being forced off his land at gunpoint.. and much, much more.

Of all the books I have listed in my resources; this is the one I most want you to read. It's a reae eye opener.

The basic thesis of the book is that will never be a lasting peace in Israel unless it is based on a lasting justice.

Also in the book he spoke of a vision he had that an Institution be established in Jerusalem that would seek truth. leaders from all over the world that had suffered war and came to peace would come to the Institution and tell how they establish.

I though this vision of would never happen. I thought it was more of an ideal than a vision. Even so; if it helped him sleep better at night, so be it.

Wow! How wrong I was. I don't think I have ever been so wrong about anything in my life as I was wrong about this.

His vision became a reality, and "SABEEL" was born. You are about to read is an example of what can be done if your heart it right. It is nothing short of a miracle. (Act of God).

The Significance of Jerusalem for Christians and of Christians for Jerusalem

*An International Conference sponsored by
Sabeel Liberation Theology Centre,
in consultation with the Middle East Council of Churches
and other ecumanical Christian organizations*

Conference Message

In Jerusalem, on 22-27 January 1996, over 300 Christians-Palestinians and international participants from more than 25 countries, lay people and clergy, including church leaders or their representatives—met to consider the theme "The Significance of Jerusalem for Christians and of Christians for Jerusalem." We gathered under the auspices of Sabeel Liberation Theology Center.

We, the conference participants, discussed the theological, spiritual, legal, political, social and cultural aspects of Jerusalem. We reaffirmed that Jerusalem should serve as the capital for two sovereign and independent states, Israel and Palestine.

Furthermore, the Palestinian Christians gathered stressed their unity with Palestinian Muslims in striving for peace and the establishment of a sovereign state in their homeland, with Jerusalem as its capital.

We worshipped together in Jerusalem, and visited a number of villages in the West Bank, so that we could meet and pray with Palestinian Christians who are prevented from entering Jerusalem. We witnessed the effects of 29 years of occupation on Palestinian society: land expropriation, new settlements and the expansion of existing ones, roadblocks preventing free movement of Palestinians, and continued detention of political prisoners (especially women, the sick and the elderly). We were appalled by the effects of the closure of Jerusalem on Palestinian life. As a result of its illegal annexation by Israel, East Jerusalem has been cut off from its natural surrounding environment and access to it has been denied to Palestinian Christians and Muslims of the West Bank and Gaza. This closure has been strictly enforced since 1993, strangling normal life in East Jerusalem itself and depriving Palestinians of its rich spiritual, cultural, medical and economic resources.

In the light of these discussions and experiences, we insist on the following:

1. The government of Israel should remove forthwith all roadblocks and obstacles preventing free access to Jerusalem for Palestinians.
2. There should be an immediate cessation of all land expropriation in the West Bank, including East Jerusalem and of the building and expansion of Jewish settlements there, notably the Jebel Abu Ghneim (Har Homa) settlement
3. The government of Israel should change its planning policies so that Palestinians have equal rights to build housing in Jerusalem and develop their institutions which have been restncted since 1967.
4. East Jerusalem, as an integral part of the occupied territories, should be included in all political arrangements relating to these territories, including self determination, release of prisoners, right of return and eventual sovereignty.

The participants visited with Palestinian Arab Christians in Israel, especially the Galilee, and affirmed their demand that equal rights and opportunities for Palestinian Arabs living in the state of Israel be granted.

The conference participants commit themselves to respect the noble ideals of all religions and dissociate themselves from all fundamentalist tendencies which subvert the dignity of people under the pretext of an alleged divine mandate. The participants repudiate the ideology and activities of Christian Zionist groups and others who seek to sanctify exclusive Israeli control over the Holy City through such campaigns as "Jerusalem 3000".

Palestinian Christians affirm their essential attachment to the Holy City and acknowledge its significance for Muslims, Christians and Jews. The international participants affirm their attachment to the Holy City and the Church of Jerusalem, the Mother Church of all Christian believers, and express their concern for the welfare of Palestinian Christians (the Living Stones, 1. Peter 2:5). In this light, we pledge to do all we can to maintain a vital Christian presence in the Holy Land. Moreover, we call on all peoples involved in the current Middle East peace talks to seriously consider this conference message.

We, both local and international Christians, recognize our responsibility to witness to the Lord Jesus Christ in the land of his birth, death and resurrection. We pray for the Peace of Jerusalem.

28 January 1996

Sabeel Solidarity Statement April 13, 2002
A CHALLENGE FROM PALESTINE UNDER FIRE

This statement was adopted by participants in the international Sabeel Solidarity Visit held in Jerusalem from April 6-13, 2002.

We have arrived in a land under its most intense military occupation in years, and among a people suffering a sustained and brutal military assault. Violence against the Palestinian people has reached a level that is unprecedented in 35 years of Israeli occupation of the West Bank, Gaza, and East Jerusalem.

Illegal Israeli settlements cover much of their land. Hundreds of Israeli checkpoints and roadblocks choke off movement by Palestinians, as well as international visitors, humanitarian aid workers, and journalists.

The people of Palestine feel betrayed by the United States, the European Union, the United Nations, the people of Israel, and the international community. The world has remained largely silent as Palestinians' land has been confiscated, their homes demolished, their culture compromised, their economy devastated, and their most basic human rights violated.

Now they stand on the brink of a disaster as terrible as the one that forced them from their homes and land in 1948. Still the world's silence betrays a people who seek justice, dignity, and their own nation.

We believe that justice for the people of Palestine demands an immediate end to Israel's occupation. Only justice can lead to lasting peace and, ultimately, to reconciliation.

We condemn all attacks on civilians, Palestinian or Israeli. Terrorism by any individual, organization or state is unacceptable to all civilized people. We see in the occupation the source of all of the violence.

We call for the establishment of a sovereign and viable Palestinian state on the whole of the Gaza Strip and West Bank, including East Jerusalem, to exist alongside

THE 5TH INTERNATIONAL SABEEL CONFERENCE STATEMENT "CHALLENGING CHRISTIAN ZIONISM"

"Blessed are the peacemakers for they shall be called the children of God."
(Matthew 5:9)

Christian Zionism is a modern theological and political movement that embraces the most extreme ideological positions of Zionism, thereby becoming detrimental to a just peace within Palestine and Israel. The Christian Zionist programme provides a worldview where the Gospel is identified with the ideology of empire, colonialism, and militarism. In its extreme form, it places an emphasis on apocalyptic events leading to the end of history rather than living Christ's love and justice today. We also repudiate the more insidious form of Christian Zionism pervasive in the mainline churches that remains silent in the face of the Israeli occupation of Palestine.

Therefore, we categorically reject Christian Zionist doctrines as a false teaching that undermines the biblical message of love, mercy, and justice.

We further reject the contemporary alliance of Christian Zionist leaders and organizations with extremist elements in the governments of Israel and the United States that are presently seeking to impose their unilateral preemptive strategies and militaristic rule over others, including Palestine and Iraq.

As a result of the 14 April, 2004 Bush-Sharon memorandum of understanding, the crisis in Israel and Palestine has moved into a new phase of oppression of the Palestinian people. This will inevitably lead to unending cycles of violence and counter violence that are already spreading throughout the Middle East and other parts of the world.

We reject the heretical teachings of Christian Zionism that facilitate and support these extremist policies as they advance a form of racial exclusivity and perpetual war rather than the gospel of universal love, redemption and reconciliation taught by Jesus Christ.

Rather than condemn the world to the doom of Armageddon we call upon everyone to liberate themselves from ideologies of militarism and occupation and instead to pursue the healing of the world. We call upon Christians in churches on every continent to prayerfully remember the suffering of the Palestinian and Israeli people, both of whom are victims of policies of occupation and militarism. These policies are reviving a system of apartheid that is turning Palestinian cities, towns and villages into impoverished ghettos surrounded by exclusively Jewish colonies. The recent construction of the Israeli wall on Palestinian land precludes a viable Palestinian state.

Therefore, we commit ourselves to the following principles as an alternative way (Sabeel):

☐ We affirm that all people are created in the image of God and called to honor the dignity and respect the equal rights of every human being.

☐ We call upon people of good will everywhere to reject the theology of Christian Zionism and all parallel religious and ideological fundamentalisms that privilege particular people at the expense of others.

☐ We are committed to the power of non-violent resistance to defeat the occupation and attain a just and lasting peace.

☐ With renewed urgency we warn that the theology of Christian Zionism is leading to the moral justification of empire, colonization, apartheid, and oppression.

☐ Moreover, we affirm that a just and lasting peace in Palestine and Israel must be based on the *Jerusalem Sabeel Document: Principles for a Just Peace in Palestine-Israel (2004)*.

Sabeel's vision embraces two sovereign states, Palestine and Israel, which will enter into confederation or even a federation, possibly with other neighboring countries, where Jerusalem becomes the federal capital. Indeed, the ideal and best solution has always been to envisage ultimately a bi-national state in Palestine-Israel where people are free and equal, living under a constitutional democracy that protects and guarantees all their rights, responsibilities, and duties without racism or discrimination-one state for two nations and three religions.

This is where Sabeel takes its stand. We will stand for justice. We can do no other. Justice alone guarantees a peace that will lead to reconciliation and a life of security and prosperity for all the peoples of our land. By standing on the side of justice, we open ourselves to the work of peace—and working for peace makes us children of God.

God demands that justice be done. No enduring peace, security, or reconciliation is possible without the foundation of justice. The demands of justice will not disappear. The struggle for justice must be pursued diligently and persistently but non-violently.

"What does the Lord require of you, to act justly, to love mercy, and to walk humbly with your God."

(Micah 6:8)

SABEEL'S 6TH INTERNATIONAL CONFERENCE STATEMENT
November 2-9, 2006

Sabeel's 6th International Conference was held November 2-9, 2006 under the theme of the *FORGOTTEN FAITHFUL—a Window into the Life and Witness of Christians in the Holy Land.* Meetings were held in various venues starting in Jerusalem and including Bethlehem, Jericho, Ramallah, and Nazareth. It was a truly ecumenical experience. The cumulative number of international and local participants in the different settings was more than 500. Approximately 200 people from 29 countries came from abroad.

Most of the speakers were local Palestinian Christians. The Orthodox Patriarch gave the initial greetings at the opening celebration and the Latin Patriarch gave a presentation on the topic of "Palestinian Christianity: The Challenges and the Vision for the Future." In addition, Archbishops and Bishops from the Orthodox, Armenian, Coptic, Syrian, Latin, Maronite, Anglican, and Lutheran churches addressed the conference. The conference also included prayers, songs, and chants from the various church traditions presented by clergy, church choirs, and soloists.

In addition to the 40 lectures given during the conference, there were special greetings given by the Governor of Jericho and the Mayors of Bethlehem, Ramallah, and Nazareth.

Furthermore, the participants worshiped in and visited 32 churches in 13 villages and came in contact with more than 50 clergy of the various church denominations in the different towns and villages. They experienced fellowship with their local sisters and brothers and had a taste of Palestinian hospitality in the meals they shared. In both Ramallah and Nazareth special cultural events were presented by young local musicians and performers who are keeping Palestinian arts alive and vibrant.

An important feature of the conference was the presentation of a survey of the Christians of the Holy Land conducted specially for Sabeel. The survey covered the areas of the West Bank, including East Jerusalem, as well as Israel. Due to political instability in Gaza, it was impossible to complete the survey there. Various aspects of the survey were analyzed by a team of professors from the Bethlehem University.

Two highlights of the conference were the opening lecture by Christian Qur'anic scholar Dr. Kenneth Cragg and the series of Bible studies presented by Dr. Kenneth Bailey in which he examined three parables in light of their cultural context and their meaning today.

Special mention must be made of the opening celebration of the conference in which the Greek Orthodox Patriarch Theophilos III welcomed and greeted the participants. A message from the General Secretary of the World Council of Churches, the Rev. Dr.

Samuel Kobia, was read. Through power point, music, song, and dance, the opening celebration reminded the participants of the origins of the Christian Faith. It emphasized the death and resurrection of Christ and the coming of the Holy Spirit at Pentecost.

Through the power of the Spirit, the Church came into being and the Gospel of freedom and love was spread from Jerusalem to the various parts of the world.

POINTS OF EMPHASIS

1. The Palestinian Christians are the descendants of the first community of believers who loved, believed in, and followed Jesus Christ. From the beginning they were a mixture of many ethnic and racial groups but all became members of the One Body of Christ, the Church.

2. In spite of the vicissitudes of history, they have maintained their faith in Christ during the last 2000 years amidst excruciating circumstances and in spite of the religious and political upheavals. Yet they have preserved the beautiful mosaic of their rich liturgical traditions and continue to bear witness. In order to strengthen the Christian presence and witness, it is mandatory, therefore, for Palestinian Christians to work together ecumenically. The hierarchies of the churches have a great responsibility to rise above denominationalism and commit themselves to nourishing closer bonds of love and acceptance among themselves.

3. Due to political and economic instability, many Palestinian Christians have been emigrating to the West. Internal as well as external factors have undermined their presence. Those who are in the Holy Land today make up less than 2% of the population.

4. Palestinian Christians are an integral part of the Palestinian people. They share the same aspirations and destiny as their Muslim sisters and brothers. All Palestinians in the West Bank and Gaza have been living under an illegal Israeli occupation for almost 40 years. With many peace-loving people from around the world, whether faith-based or secular, Muslims and Christians continue to work for the end of the Israeli occupation and the establishment of a viable, independent and sovereign state in Palestine.

5. The Israeli Arab community—Christian and Muslim—continues to struggle for total equality with its

Jewish counterpart. The obstacle, however, is the nature of the state of Israel. It is a Jewish state and not a state for all its citizens. Therefore, the struggle will continue until total equality is achieved.

6. Participants also observed the daily suffering of Palestinians in the West Bank and East Jerusalem and were acutely aware of the plight of Gazans, about 80 of whom (half of them civilians) were killed during the week of the conference. Conference participants were shocked by news of the Israeli army attack on an apartment building in Beit Hanoun in the Gaza Strip that resulted in the deaths of 19 civilians, primarily women and children. Moreover, during the conference day in Bethlehem, participants were unable to visit the Church of Nativity or to view the Wall in central Bethlehem because of funerals being held for 2 Palestinians who had been killed and had their family homes demolished by the Israeli army. Special prayers were raised for the victims and their families.

7. It was clear to participants that Palestinians and Israelis—Christians, Muslims, and Jews can live together in peace. The greatest obstacle to genuine reconciliation, however, stems from Israel's refusal to accept Palestinian rights to a state of their own within the 1967 borders, i.e. all of the West Bank including East Jerusalem and the Gaza Strip. The conference called for strong response against the Israeli government policies of confiscation of Palestinian land in the West Bank, building and expanding of settlements, the presence of hundreds of checkpoints, and the building of the segregation Wall which separates Palestinians from Palestinians and takes their land and water. All these measures are eroding the possibility of the two state solution to the conflict.

8. Such obstacles to peace must be actively resisted both locally and internationally through nonviolent methods like boycotts and Morally Responsible Investment. Moreover,

international sanctions that make life untenable for people in the occupied territories must be immediately lifted.

9. Palestinian Christians have a mandate from Christ to be salt of the earth and light of the world. They have a vocation to remain in the land and maintain a prophetic voice for justice, peace, and reconciliation.

The conference ended on the shores of the Sea of Galilee with a Communion Service and the commissioning of the participants to commit themselves to strive for peace with justice. Sabeel calls on all our friends:

1. To establish bonds of fellowship with Palestinian Christians and to stand in solidarity with all Palestinians in their struggle for liberation.
2. To commit themselves to active prayer, education, and advocacy on behalf of the Palestinian people
3. To campaign for truth and justice with the energy and consistency of an everflowing stream
4. To work without ceasing to bring healing and reconciliation to all people with God's joy and peace in their hearts, especially to the people of the land where the first message of peace was proclaimed.

Sabeel, Jerusalem
November 15, 2006

At it's inception, Sabeel was a grass roots organization with little recognition and as a new grass roots organization, it's future was unknown; perhaps even doubtful.

That isn't so anymore. Each year Sabeel grew stronger and stronger and continued to gather more International attention and greater participation from National representatives from all over the World.

Today, Sabeel is a very strong organization with chapters all over the world and Sabel has impact all over the world.

More and more Countries around the Globe are becoming aware of the Israeli/Palestinian conflict and are acting together to bring about a lasting peace in the region.

Chapter 11

The Fifty-Year War

This Chapter is an excerpt from a PBS documentary with their permission to allow me to print what follows. Palestine—a land divided, a holy place, a battleground, claimed by both the Arabs and Jews. Part One—Land Divided 1947-1956. By 1947, the lines were drawn. To the Jews, Palestine is their traditional and spiritual home, the Promised Land. That the majority of the inhabitants are Arabs, they too regard Palestine as their rightful home, but with the end of the war, into Palestine's ports came ship after ship crammed full of illegal immigrants, refugees of recent persecution from Germany, Austria, Poland, Berlin, and Dahaw. The Arabs, fearful of becoming a minority, persuaded the British to limit Jewish immigration. Jewish extremist's attacked British troops, wrecked government buildings, blew up trains and ships, and so Palestine remains a place of martial law where all go their way under watch where the innocent suffer with the guilty.

Great Britain had ruled Palestine for three decades. Lord Cadogan, UK delegate to the UN, speaks "After years of strenuous effort, his majesty's government has reached the conclusion that they are not able to bring about a settlement of Palestine based on the consent of both Arabs and Jews and that the mandate is no longer workable."

Palestine—Arrival of UN Fact-Finders. A York transport landing at Liverpool Airport brings delegates to the UN special committee on Palestine. The UN committee considered the partition of Palestine as an Arab State. But the Arabs did not want to talk to the committee. They wanted nothing to do with the Jews.

Hazem Nusseibeh (Palestine broadcasting Service), "If the Jews want to take Palestine from us, I swear that we will throw them into the sea." (And he pointed to the Mediterranean, a few hundred meters from the place we had gathered.) The Arab leadership believed that if a partition was opposed, they could resist it by force.

Jamael Hussien, the chairman of the Arab higher committee said, "Only four to five hundred riflemen can easily take over Tel-Ave."

Largest immigrant ship seized—while the committee was still in Palestine, a ship called Exodus arrived in Hifa, loaded with Jewish Holocaust survivors. She had on board some five thousand Jews who hoped to enter Palestine illegally. When she was boarded at sea by the Navy, a fierce battle was fought on her decks, resulting in many casualties on both sides. The UN committee saw firsthand the immigrants' despair when they were forced to return to Europe. The Jews argued that the refugees needed a home and that they would not be welcomed by an Arab state. The UN committee agreed. They recommended that Palestine be partitioned when the British pulled out.

Mohsein Abdek Khalek (Palestinian student) "We felt that what had happened to the Palestinians was unjust, and that the division of Palestine was not fair."

The Arabs were outraged. Abel Sabit (King Farouk's cousin, Egypt), "We had a gentleman who managed to penetrate, literally into the circle of the Security Council, to read a letter written in the blood of several thousand Egyptian Muslim brothers, denouncing Israel and the support of Israel."

"You all know how to vote. Those in favor will say yes, those who are against will say no."

"Yair Zaban (High School student, Jerusalem) No one relied on the calculations made by the president of the assembly. Each person took his own pencil and piece of paper and calculated whether there was two-thirds for the partisan or not. *United Kingdom—abstain. United States—yes. Uruguay—yes. Venezuela . . . And toward the end, during the last countries, USA, Venezuela, etc., we found there was two-thirds.* We jumped from our places with joy. We wept, we kissed." The resolutions of this committee for Palestine was adopted by thirty-three votes for, thirteen against, and ten abstain.

Meir Pail, Palestinian Jew, "I was glad, I was very glad, because for me, it was important that the U N according the Decree of Nations, was giving/granting the Jews, I'd say the Zionists, an independent country on the land of Israel, and I thought in my heart history is turning a huge page."

Hazem Nusseibeh, Palestine Broadcasting Service, "The news was broadcast at 8:00 p.m. The Palestinian people listened to it everywhere, and there was this feeling of frustration and sadness—a feeling of catastrophe that was about to befall Palestine. Riots and demonstrations started everywhere." Arabs attacked Jews and the Jews hit back. Cities and neighborhoods were divided amongst religious lines. In Jerusalem, an Arab car bomb destroyed the Jewish agency offices, seven were killed, more than one hundred wounded. The fifty years war was underway.

Palestinian forces from towns and villages along the road to Jerusalem were commanded by Abdul Kador El Hussien. They blocked supplies going from Jewish, held Tel Aviv to a besieged Jerusalem. Keeping the Jew in Jerusalem supplied was the first priority of the Jewish army. They tried to defend the convoys.

Uzi Narkiss, Palmach Officer, "It was very hard to protect the convoys. We had a huge amount of casualties amongst the convey escorts, and there was a big waste of product.

Yitzhak Navon, Haganah Intelligence Officer," When a convoy got through, the whole city knew. The trucks brought vital supplies . . . flour. We really needed matches and cigarettes. Can you imagine soldiers without cigarettes? We were kept alive by the convoy from Tel Aviv."

Yitzhak Rabin, Haganah Brigade Commander, "We started with military operations to make sure that the road between Tel Aviv and Jerusalem would not be endangered by the big villages of towns that were along the road where from came all the attacks on the convoys. A special Haganah Brigade was formed to open the road to Jerusalem. The system was to protect the village, to give warning to the civilians, to destroy the village, and by the elimination of the villages alone and adjacent to the road, we were sure there would be no attacks."

The Jews tried to seize Kastill, a village controlling the road to Jerusalem.

Uzi Narkiss, Palmach Officer, "It was a Palmach unit, my troops that captured the Kastrell, and it was here that Abdul Kabal El Hussien, the Palestinian leader, was killed. Hussien's soldiers went to recover the body of their leader. The Arabs counter attacked. Our reinforcements were wiped out. It was a very black day."

Down the road from Kastrell, there would be another battle that day. Two Jewish extremist organizations, Irgun and Lehi, who had each fought the British, were eager to prove themselves in the new war. It was such a tragedy. Deir Yassin was a lovely village. The events at Deir Yassin would haunt relations between Jews and Arabs for years to come. Deir Yassin had stayed out of the fighting. It was not on the Haganah's list of hostile villages.

Meir Pail, Haganah Officer, "I ran into a man who had left us for the terrorists. He told me that the Irgun and Leaky had gotten permission from our commander to attack the village of Deir Yassin. He was very proud."

Ben Zion Cohen, Irgun Commander, "The Irgun and Lehi forces were ordered to take Deir Yassin."

Meir Pail, Haganah Officer, "I ran to my commander and asked, 'why did you allow it?' He said, 'I suggested two other targets, they turned them down.' He said, 'I can't shoot them, can I?' So I decided to spy on them."

Abu Mahmoud, president of Deir Yassin, "Their loud speakers blared out, lay down your arms. Run for your lives. I was kneeling down like this, when I looked up I saw the village ablaze. Their attack lit up the whole village." The village was not the soft target the Jews had expected.

Ben Zion Cohen, Raid Commander, "From the windows of their houses, Arabs were shooting at our soldiers, and from a force of 132, we had forty-two wounded and six dead. The commander ordered a house to house attack. So I gave the order. Before entering a house, throw a couple of grenades inside."

Abu Mohmoud, "they threw a grenade into one house, twenty-eight were killed."

Ezra Yakhin, Lehi fighter, "It was impossible to attack the enemy without hurting their families. It was difficult. It was painful, and I am sorry we had to do it, but we had no choice."

Abu Mohmoud, "After the battle they took fourteen prisoners. They lined them up at the quarry and mowed them down. They threw their bodies in the quarry. That's what happened."

Ben Zion Cohen, "While this was going on, Jews came from the next village. Most of them were religious, by the way. They started yelling, Bastards! Murderers! What are you doing? Some shouted in Hebrew, others in Yiddish. 110 Arabs died in Deir Yassin. Some died fighting, others were murdered. The survivors were taken to Jerusalem."

Abu Mohmoud, "We gathered at Jerusalem at the Hebron gate. We checked who was missing and who had survived. Then the Palestinian leaders arrived, including Dr. Kalede."

Hazem Nusseibeh, Palestine Broadcasting Service, "I asked Dr. Kalede, How we should cover the story? He said 'we should make the most of this, so he wrote a press release stating that at Deir Yassin, children were murdered, pregnant women were raped, all sorts of atrocities.'" Arab radio stations passed on the false reports, ignoring the protests of the witnesses.

Abu Mohmoud, "We said there was no rape. He said we have to say this so that Arab armies will come and liberate Palestine from the Jews."

Hazem Nusseibeh, "This was our biggest mistake. We did not know how our people would react. As soon as they heard that women had been raped at Deir Yassin, Palestinians fled in terror. They ran away from all our villages. In the next few months, over half the population of the Arab people, over percent of a million people fled their homes in Palestine. Israel never allowed them back. The British did little to prevent the atrocities committed by both sides. As they prepared to leave, they washed their hands of the whole mess."

At the United Nations, the Jews announced their plans. "Not later than May 16 next, a provisional Jewish government will commence to function, in cooperation with the representatives of the United Nations then in Palestine." The Jewish leaders sought political support abroad. David Ben Gurion, Jewish leader, "The U.S. State dept argued against it. Their first response was, 'no country, no state.'" Ben Gurion sent his close colleague, Mosa Sharett, to convince the Americans to recognize the proposed Jewish state. Sharett tried to persuade Secretary of State George Marshall who was totally opposed to the idea.

Gideon Rafael, Sharett's aide, "Sharett explained that we had no other way than to proceed, this is an historic juncture, *if* we miss that, we may create a tragedy for future generations." But President Truman surprised everyone with his strong support. "I was told by all these so called experts that if it was done, it would involve the whole Mid-East war and it would involve the United States. Hitler had been murdering Jews right and left, I saw it and I dream about it even to this day. The Jews needed someplace where they could go. It is my attitude that the American government could not stand idly by while the victims of Milter's madness are not allowed to build new lives."

Marshall was worried that war would break out. "We are in the midst of a very critical situation. We should therefore carefully avoid approaching international problems on an emotional basis." He wanted to maintain good relations with the Arabs.

Adel Sabit, King Farouk's cousin, Egypt, "I was on the receiving end of Ezempaches impressions of his meeting with Marshall. I mean he was happy and he felt much more reassured about the Americans, after having talked to Marshall than before. We have the sovrentry with us; they were our partners in this meeting."

Two days before the British left Palestine, Truman summoned Marshall to the White House. Clark Clifford was asked to support the case for a Jewish State. Clark Clifford, counsel to the president, "Senator Marshall started off and the president listened attentively, and then said 'I would like now to hear from Clark.' But as I spoke, I saw Marshall's face getting redder and redder. When I finished, he exploded. Marshall accused Truman of a transparent dodge to win the Jewish vote."

Abba Eban, Jewish representative to the United States. "Clark Clifford did not disguise the fact that Marshall was stark raving mad. They don't need a State, they don't deserve a State, it isn't theirs, and they have stolen that land. These were Marshall's words. He turned to the president. He said I'm obliged, Mr. President, to tell you that if you should adopt the policy that is recommended by Clifford, I would be unable to vote for you in this upcoming election in November. Well, dead silence in the room. No one had ever heard anything like that. I had never heard anyone threaten the president of the United States in that manner. Before Marshall could go any further, Truman ended the meeting. I gathered my papers together, and the president said "that was tough as a cob!"

Gideon Rafael, Sharett's aide, "Marshall said to Sharett, 'it's your decision and don't count that we can bail you out, but, eh, we know you have reached an historic stage, and, eh, God protect you.'"

Trans-Jordon, Paramount News

Eastward, the Arab legion poised for invasion on the Trans-Jordon border. The rarely photographed King Abdullah reviewed a set of reinforcements from Iraq. Marshall's prediction of war was about to come true. Five Arab states mobilized on the border, threatening to enter Palestine and crush a Jewish State if it came into being.

Tel Aviv, Last Day of British Rule, May 14, 1948

For the Jews in Palestine, this was a critical moment. Ben Gurion was determined to go on with or without international support. David Ben Gurion, "I had to act fast. I did not consult anyone. Today, the British Mandate over the land of Israel ends. I declare a Jewish State in the ancient lands of Israel. It will be called the State of Israel." At the same time, the UN's role in Palestine was supposed to end. When the hands pointed at six o'clock, the Iraqi delegate got up and said, "Mr. President, there is a very important matter to consider before we proceed. It is one minute past six. Indeed, I think it is two minutes. The United States delegate, when he came to this roster, declared that if by six o'clock, we cannot arrive at any conclusion, the war game is up, and I hold that to you, Mr. President, to start the voting. The time is past six now."

Abba Eban, Jewish representative to the United States, "This was the only indication that the Iraqi delegate and I ever agreed on anything. He was full of exuberance because he thought the game is up and now the road is open for the Arab invasion. I felt the game is up. That meant we were free to establish our State without being accused of impinging on an international decision." Then, the news came from Israel arrived.

U.S. delegate Jessup, "This government has been informed that a Jewish State has been proclaimed in Palestine and recognition has been requested by the provisional government thereof. The United States recognizes the provisional government as the de facto authority of the new State of Israel."

Abba Eban: "Scarcely had the United States pronounced its words of recognition, and almost unnoticed by Arab delegation which were still celebrating our American victory, Andrew Gramico rose and uh said, 'the Soviet Union, that unlike the Western powers which had abandoned the Jewish people to its dark and fearful fate, the Soviet Union recognizes the State of Israel, and therefore, I would say the issue of Israel's recognition was solved almost miraculously within a few hours of our independence declaration.'"

After two hundred years of exile, Jewish people had a state of their own. But even as they danced, Israel's fate hung in the balance. The day after Ben Gurion declared the State of Israel, Jordon, Iraq, Lebanon, and Syria invaded. But the largest Arab army had only been tested on the parade ground. At its head was the playboy, King Farouk.

Adel Sabit, King Farouk's cousin, Egypt: "The king hadn't had any experience at war. Nobody did really, including the chief of the Egyptian Army, you see. At the time, euphoria ran through the outer ranks. The boys were very pleased with the war. They thought it was a good idea, but they had no idea of the logistics and problems they were going to face." Still, the Arab States with a population of over forty million looked certain to overwhelm Israel's *Vi* million Jews. It seemed Ben Gurion's State would last only a few days. Adel Sabit, "We thought it was going to be a pushover that the Jews were going to run away the moment they saw Arab regular Army in uniform moving upon them, armed with bayonets and whatever."

Egypt's army attacking from the south headed toward the main Jewish center, Tel Aviv. Jordon's Arab legion took the West Bank and the old city of Jerusalem, The Syrians moved toward Nazareth, while the Lebanese attacked from the north. The Arab regular armies converged on Palestine superior in numbers and equipment. Early in the war, they had a number of victories. Whenever they overran Israeli villages, the inhabitants were either expelled or killed. The Egyptian army was finally halted only twenty miles from Tel Aviv. The Israelis were fighting for their survival, and after three weeks of fierce resistance, they brought the Arabs to a standstill.

Yitzhak Navon, Israeli Army Officer, "We had no aircraft, we had no tanks, and we were going into war this way. We hardly even had guns. We would try to buy guns as much we could. Anywhere we could. In this situation, we were really saved by Czechoslovakia, that is Russia. America didn't give us arms."

Adel Sabot, "When the weapons came in, the whole balance of power changed and the Israelis could then pass on to the offensive."

Zachariah Muhieddin, Egyptian Officer, "We weren't even mentally prepared. We just weren't ready. So our officers were confused and panic stricken."

Yitzhak Navon, "So then the Egyptian army was surrounded, and then the Jordanian army just kept neutral . . . didn't interfere in any way. Finally, our prime minister here in Egypt was murdered by the Muslim brothers, and his successor said, 'There is no future in this war, let's make peace.'" But there was no peace, only a cease-fire agreement. The Arabs believed a peace treaty would be an acknowledgment of defeat.

February 24, 1949

Both sides mourned their dead. Even before the cease-fire agreements were signed, Israel held its first democratic election. Ben Gurion and his labor party won. Israel celebrated the triumph of its armed forces, but the Arabs refused to recognize Israel's right to exist. For the Arabs, the legacy of the forty-eight war was the displacement of the Palestine people. The Palestinians now faced political extinction. The West Bank was annexed by Jordan, and Gaza was ruled by Egypt. Egypt, the most powerful Arab country, was shaken by the defeat. A group of young officers, frustrated by the incompetence of the king and the new prime minister, plotted a coup.

Anwar Sadat, Free Officers Movement, "I went to the prime minister and delivered the ultimatum to him. He was shocked. Believe me, because, up till this moment he did not know we were going to dethrone the king at all. He was shocked. He looked at me like this.

"I told him yes.

"He asked, 'Are you powerful enough?'

"I told yes.

"Go ahead and deliver it to the king. He must leave by six o'clock this evening."

Egyptian Coup D'etat-July 23, 1952

From Cairo, came these first authentic pictures of the bloodless coup by which the Army took over control of Egypt. It was the end of the king's attempt to control power. Zachariah Muhieddin, Free Officers Movement, "As we took the king away, he said, 'You ate me for lunch before I could eat you for dinner.'"

Egypt's new leader, Gemal Abdel Nasser, pledged radical reform, "There were six principals to put an end to colonialism, to put an end to fatalism, to put an end to corrupt exploitation by capitalism."

David Ben Gurion, prime minister, Israel, "I read that Nasser was going to Yugoslavia. I thought President Tito could help make peace. I knew a friend of Tito's. I asked him to go to Yugoslavia. I said, 'Get Tito to ask Nasser if he will make peace.'"

Shimon Peres, Ben Gurion's advisor, "Tito passed on the message. Nasser said that if he was seen talking to Israel, he might even be killed."

Sharett, Ben Gurion's foreign minister, attacks. Ziamah Divon, Israeli diplomat, "Sharett believed the best way to ensure the security of Israel, was to understand the Arabs and negotiate peace." Sharett sent Divon to Paris, the UN General Assembly's temporary home.

Divon, "I told a friend I was ordered to Paris to meet Arabs, and he said, 'Ziamah, I know you like Cervantes, but I never saw you as Don Quixote. Will you go to the Plaque de Concordre and shout, "Any Arabs here?"'"

Abdel Rahman Sadek, Egyptian diplomat, "I was sitting on the balcony of the UN. A young man came in and sat next to me. We began to talk. I said to him, 'My dear, sir, I am a Jew. I looked at him in his face. I saw no sign of embarrassment.' So I asked him, 'Who do you represent?' When I pressed him, he said, 'Sharett.'"

Divon, "I said I am an Israeli that dreams of a peace with Egypt." For Egyptians, talking to Israelis was taboo.

So Abdel Rahman Sadek, who was nervous when he was summoned by Nasser, "I went in and found Nasser standing in the room. He said 'I want to tell you that you have my permission to continue the talks with the Israeli in Paris.'" The diplomats' reports were to be for Nasser's ears only. "He said, 'I want you to see if there is a chance of avoiding bloodshed.'"

Divon, "While we conducted the talks with Abdel Rahman, there was once in a while a radical escalation of Egyptian statements about Israel. An Egyptian leader even said that Israel was the cancer in the midst of the Arab world, and we asked them to refrain from such inflammatory language."

Nasser's envoy returned to Paris with promises to tone down the anti-Israeli propaganda on Cairo radio and to restrain the guerilla raids against Israel. But Nasser would not terminate the war, nor would he establish diplomatic relations or allow Israeli ships through the Suez Canal and the Straits of Tehran. Sharett was disappointed.

Divon, "Sharett's message said that they were sorry, of course that the Egyptian government would not change its official policy, which was a clear anti-Israeli policy."

Sharett's repeated offers to start peace negotiations were turned down.

Sadek, "I had realized that the Israelis continued to say they want peace. I realized also that the Arabs refused to talk."

Israel desperately needed peace. Jewish refugees from Europe and Arab countries were streaming in. Its population doubled in the first two years. Its economy was in ruins. New immigrants were often settled along Israel's frontiers. They lived in fear of frequent Arab raids. Ben Gurion blamed Nasser for the raids. He ordered the Israeli army to strike Arab countries harboring infiltrators.

Shimon Peres, Ben Gurion's advisor, "Ben Gurion knew Arab villages supported these terrorists. We had to show them that helping terrorists was dangerous and to protect our settlements."

Ariel Sharon, Commander, Anti-terrorist Unit, "I was called to see Mosha Dian. A mother had been killed, murdered on a settlement. The murderers left tracks which led to a village across the border in Jordan. My orders were to reach a village in Jordan.

We had to blow up as many buildings as possible and cause as many Arab casualties as possible."

Israel-Jordan Border Clash! Warner Pathe News

The tiny village of Kibia on the Israel and Jordan border is in ruins, as day survivors relate how troops struck across the frontier at night. They accuse the Israeli forces of leveling buildings with grenades, shellfire, and explosives, trapping entire families in the rubble. The attack prompts the United States, England, and France to deliver their sharpest rebuke to Israel since its founding and to demand stern action to punish the guilty troops.

Sharon, "After the operation, I was called to see Ben Gurion. It was the first time I had met him."

Ben Gurion, "Sharon, what do I think about him? He's a nice boy! And a good soldier!"

Sharon, "He said one thing to me. He said, 'It doesn't matter what the world says. It doesn't matter what they say about Israel anywhere else. The only thing that matters is that we can exist here. Unless it is clear that there is a price to pay for Jewish lives, we will not be able to survive, and that's what counts.'" Ben Gurion was such a believer in the importance of agricultural settlements that he abandoned the prime ministership and joined a kibbutz in the dessert. He was succeeded by Sharett, who hoped he could advance Israeli security though diplomacy. But his minister of Defense, Slavon, believed in military solutions. In July 1954, the British announced they were quitting their huge military base on the Suez Canal.

Benjamin Givli, Director of Military Intelligence, Israel, "We feared we would be exposed to an attack from Egypt. The fact that the British army was there served as a buffer. It reduced the chance of an Egyptian attack."

On his own, Levon ordered his own plans for destabilizing Egypt and frightening the British into remaining. Levon summoned the Director of Military Intelligence to his home in Tel Aviv. Levon would not stop talking about the need for action. He suggested all sorts of schemes. We cooked up a plan to hit targets in Egypt. Levon said, "Go ahead, activate the unit."

In Egypt, Israeli military intelligence had recruited young Jews to act as saboteurs. Marcelle Ninio, Egyptian Jew, "Ai was ready to do anything to help Israel. I was idealistic. I was naive. A codeword broadcast during Israeli radio's 'housewives' choice,' was the signal to act."

Robert Dassa, Egyptian Jew, "In Cairo, I went to one cinema, my friend went to another. I put the bomb under an empty seat." No one was killed, and the saboteurs were all caught. The news was splashed all over Egyptian newspapers.

Gideon Rafael, Sharett's advisor, "So I went to Sharett and said, 'Look, urn, this is the communiqué from Cairo. What do you know about it?' And he said, 'no, no, no, this is not right. It cannot be. How can something like this happen that I the prime minister does not know about.'"

After he learned of Levon's role, Sharett's first priority was to save the lives of the young Jews. Ziamah Divon, Israeli diplomat, "Sharett called on me. He said the cabinet is worried about the prisoners in Egypt. We must prevent death sentences." In a bid for mercy, Sharett sent Divon to Paris to reveal the truth to Nasser's envoy.

Abdel Rahman Sadek, Egyptian diplomat, "Divon told me the plot was hatched in the Ministry of Defense. Sharett had no idea about it." Nasser's response was not what Sharret had hoped for. In Cairo, two of the saboteurs were executed; the others went to prison, Marcell Nina and Robert Daza, for fifteen years.

Sharett in his office that night confided to his diary that he was living in a nightmare. If I do not remove Levon, I am supporting something rotten that will destroy the Defense Ministry and army command. If I do act, it will destroy the party and cause a scandal. What should I do?

Levon was dismissed of his post as defense minister. Egypt also was playing with fire. In Gaza, it recruited and trained Palestinians for military action.

Khaled Al Ghoul, Palestinian recruit, "They paid four pounds a month, and in those days, it was a lot of money, so it was good." They were sent to Israel to gather intelligence and commit sabotage. Ghoul, "They would see if an airport was built and come back and report it. Others went on military operations and carried out attacks."

Uzi Narkiss, Israeli Army Officer, "These infiltrators were a tremendous security problem, not only for the settlers on the border, but also in the center of the country, They were attacking places not five kilometers from Tel Aviv."

Frequent attacks and the loss of lives were not only a disaster for the victims' families; they fostered a profound sense of helplessness among Israelis. The government seemed unable to protect its own people. Only one man could satisfy the public's demand for action. Within months, Ben Gurion was back as prime minister. By mid-1955, Nasser turned to the Soviet bloc for economic and military assistance. The conflict now became a part of the cold war, and Egypt received a huge arms shipment from Czechoslovakia. New tanks, artillery, bombers, and jet fighters threatened to render the Israeli army and its propeller air force, obsolete. General Mosha Dian wanted to strike at the Egyptian army before it could absorb its new weapons, but Ben Gurion felt that Israel could not fight alone.

Rafael, "Ben Gurion became more and more convinced that there could be no diplomatic solution, and because of the accumulation of arms in Egypt, we would have to stall war until we get by Egypt."

A few weeks later, President Nasser nationalized the Suez Canal. Unexpectedly, Ben Gurion found himself with two new allies. Britain and France had jointly owned the canal and wanted it back. Ben Gurion sent Shimon Perez to a secret meeting in Paris.

Perez, Director General, Defense Ministry, "The British defense minister told me Britain and France were planning a operation to take the Suez Canal back from Nasser, and he asked me would Israel join them. 'How long would it take Israeli troops to reach the canal?'" Ben Gurion waited anxiously for the return of his emissary. "Ben Gurion asked me, 'Well, what did the French say?' So I began to tell him about their plan. He interrupted and said, 'OK, this changes everything.'"

Israel invaded Egypt, secretly supported by Britain and France (October 29, 1956). Within a week, Israeli troops had captured the Sinai Desert. Britain and France tried to retake the Suez Canal, until international pressure forced them to withdraw. But for Israel, the war was a triumph.

Ben Gurion, "We achieved our main purpose. Main purpose was intimidation. The second objective was to secure safety for our settlements near the Gaza strip. I can't tell you we got it entirely, but they were more safe than they were before." The Israeli forces withdrew from Sinai and the positions along the Israeli border and the Straights of Tehran were guarded by UN forces. For ten years, there was peace between the Israeli and Egyptian boarder under the UN flag.

1967—Trouble and Death in the Middle East

Fighting erupted quickly when the Syrians allegedly fired on Israeli farmers operating tractors. Israel used tanks, mortars, and aircraft to counterattack. Israeli premier Levi Esko said, "Friendly foreign powers will understand the situation."

In May 1967, the Soviet Union took a step that would change the map of the Middle East. The losers would be their own allies. It all began with a false report from Soviet intelligence. Anwar Sadat, the speaker of the Egyptian parliament, was in Moscow for talks with Soviet Prime Minister Kosegan. It was a routine trip. Egypt was now firmly in the Soviet camp. Sadat was seen to his plane by the deputy foreign minister.

Evgeny Pyrlin, Soviet Foreign Ministry, "The minister took Sadat aside. He said Israeli troops were massing against Syria. He asked him to report this at once to Nasser." Egypt's President Nasser was the hero of the Arab world. If Israel was massing troops on the Syrian border, Nasser would be expected to act. He sent for his chief of staff and instructed him to find out what the Israelis were up to.

General Fawzi, chief of staff, Egypt, "I went to the border between Syria and Israel. I found nothing unusual. So I asked to see the latest aerial photos. They showed me photos from the previous day. I studied them—nothing."

Salah Bassiouny, Foreign Ministry, Egypt, "The chief of staff found nothing to backup the Soviet report, but then the Soviet ambassador came back to us. He said, 'Soviet intelligence has reconfirmed the report. Israeli troops really were massing on the Syrian border and the situation was very dangerous.'"

Soviet diplomats spread the alarm throughout the region, even in Israel where the prime minister and his wife soon found out.

Miriam Eshkol, Israeli prime minister's wife, "It was two thirty in the morning. A secretary came in looking sleepy. He said, 'The Soviet ambassador is down in the lobby. He is all dressed up, very formal, and he insists on seeing the prime minister right now.' I said, 'let's receive him in our pajamas.'"

Pyrlin, Soviet Foreign Ministry, "Our ambassador gave Eshkol a telegram from Kosegan. Eshkol offered to go to Moscow to discuss the regional situation."

Miriam Eshkol, "The ambassador was angry. He said, 'You are massing your troops in the North.' I said, 'We can go there now. We can go together to the Golan border. You'll see. We haven't mobilized anything.' The Soviet ambassador said no.'"

At that time, Soviet leaders believed that America was on the run in Vietnam. Some in the Kremlin now sought to weaken America's influence in the Middle East, even at the risk of another regional war. Pyrlin, "We believed a war could bring us political gains, even a stalemate could bring us benefits. Egypt had our backing, both political and military. We thought their forces would demonstrate the benefits of Soviet support. So we were confident that the balance of power in the Middle East would be altered by a localized war."

In Cairo, Nasser had put his armed forces on alert the moment he received the report. If Moscow's plan was to provoke a war, it seemed to be working.

Shams Badran, Minister of War, Egypt, "The Russian report escalated everything. We felt obliged to move troops into the Sinai. From there, we could retaliate against Israel if Israel attacked Syria."

General Fawzi, chief of staff, Egypt, "Nasser did not want a war with Israel. Abdul Nasser was thinking of his image in the Arab world. So he put on a show of strength using the armed forces. Amir wanted to attack Israeli right away." Fawzi, "The Arab media had been criticizing Nasser. Some countries had accused Nasser of hiding behind the United Nations. Since the Suez War of 1956, United Nations' troops had provided a buffer on the border between Egypt and Israel. Now, Nasser ordered them out (May 18, 1967). The eyes of the world focused on a small harbor at the edge of the Sinai desert, Sharm El Sheik."

General Noufal, "Egyptian Army Headquarters wanted to expel the troops from Sharm El Sheik. I told them if we do that, Egyptian troops would have to take over Sharm El Sheik. We would then be obliged to close the Straights of Tiran. That will mean war." A blockade at the Straights of Tiran by Egypt could lead to war because the Straights at the foot of the Gulf of Aqaba controlled Israel's only trade route to the eastern half of the world.

Nasser, in the name of Arab solidarity was going on the offensive. President Gamel Abdel Nasser, May 22, 1967, Egypt, "Our armed forces are ready for war. The Gulf of Aqaba belongs to Egypt. There is no way that we will allow Israeli ships to pass through. The Jews are threatening war. We tell them hello and welcome. We are ready for war, but there is no way we will give up our rights to the Gulf of Aqaba." In Israel, the people prepared to defend themselves. Their prime minister, Eshkol, summoned his cabinet and military commanders.

General Meir Amit, Head of Mossad, Israel, "I told him, until now, I was not sure what was going to happen, but after the Egyptians closed the Straights, I'm sure the situation will develop into a war. The Straights are a case of spelling for us, and I told him very firmly that this will be their end. This will be their grave."

General Gavish, Israeli Commander, "The commanders told him, we have no choice. We have to mobilize. We have to launch an attack within seventy-two hours. If we give the Egyptians more time, they will pack the Sinai with more and more divisions." The general saw Israel becoming increasingly vulnerable.

Abba Eban, foreign minister, Israel, "The chief of staff, General Ravin was very worried, he smokes a great number of cigarettes, ate most of the nuts and raisins in the little basket there, and he was very worried, not because he doubted the result of the war but because we were really very unprepared for war."

Rabin asked Abba Eban for a diplomatic solution. Eban, "Rabin said we were really not prepared for war and secondly there should still be an attempt to avoid it by exercising pressures and warning upon the Egyptians. Then, Mr. Eshkol sent me a note saying what are you doing here?" Eshkil dispatched Abba Eban to seek the help of Israel's key allies. He wanted an international fleet to keep the Straights open to prevent war.

May 25, 1967, Washington DC

"I have been asked by my government to explore what these governments intend to do in order to reopen this international waterway to the situation by law."

"What do you intend the United States to do, sir?" a reporter asked.

"Well, a, I've come here, really, just to find out what exactly the United States intends to do."

President Johnson made it clear that he didn't want Israel to attack first.

Robert McNamara, Defense Secretary, United States, "The president made it very clear when speaking to me, and I am going to rather crude here, get Eban in here, you know the family court is the White House, so we can work him over because we had heard that the Israelis were about to preempt. They were about to attack the Egyptians."

Walt Rostow, National Security Advisor, United States, "Eban talked at great length and eloquently. He always spoke eloquently and always at great length, but what he had to say was quite simple. This was a mortal crisis for Israel and he wanted to know what the United States was prepared to do. The president, he simply expressed skepticism about the idea that Israel was in danger. He said, 'You are not in danger. You are in a very difficult situation but you are not in peril.'"

Joseph Sisco, State Department, United States, said to Eban, "We do not believe that Egypt is about to attack Israel. Moreover, if it does, you'll lick um."

To make his point, President Johnson asked the defense department's assessment of the likely outcome of a Middle East War. We had concluded that if Israel preempted, they could win clearly in a period of about seven days as I remember. We had also estimated that if they did not preempt, and Egypt attacked first that it would take longer, perhaps ten to fourteen days. Then, the president took out a piece of paper and started reading from it as though it was some sort of sacred text and what this document said was, *Israel will not be alone unless it decides to be alone.* "Sisco, 'If you go alone, you will stand alone.'" *That was a very cold blooded statement.* "We will not come to your defense if you preempt. We cannot come to your defense if you preempt."

Israel received its warning in the White House; an Egyptian delegation was heading toward the Kremlin.

Salah Bassiouny, Foreign Ministry, Egypt, "We didn't even see Moscow. We were driven in cars with the curtains drawn straight into the Kremlin." The Egyptians were self-assured. If war came, the Egyptian military could handle it. In fact, he described the army like a wild horse, raring to go. But the Soviets warned the Egyptians not to be seen as the aggressors.

Pogol Akopov, Soviet foreign Ministry, "Prime Minister Kasigan said, 'Tell Nasser that if he strikes first, he will escalate the conflict. He will provoke the superpowers. America will not stand aside.'"

Shams Badran, Minister of War, Egypt, "I said, 'we understand, but closing the Straights isn't an attack on America.'"

The Soviets made it clear they meant what they said.

Badran, Egypt, "We asked about the arms contracts we had with them. We asked if they would hurry things up, especially since spare parts we needed for our planes. We could've taken them with us in a bag."

Akopov, "They were always asking for arms. Every high level delegation would ask for arms, including Badram"

Badran, "They did not refuse to supply the arms, they just claimed they had none.

I was really shocked. I thought, how could our Soviet friends treat us like this? War was at our doorstep."

Nasser got the message. The Soviets would back him only if he did not appear to be the aggressor. His commanders were instructed to stay on the defensive, ready to absorb an Israeli attack.

Badran, "The air force chief jumped up. He said it would be crippling. He said, 'Mr. President, the first strike will be crippling.'" He said it in English. He meant that a first strike by Israel would cripple our air force.

The commander in chief told him, "If you let them strike first, you will fight only Israel, but if you strike first, you will have to fight Israel and America."

But the war fever in Cairo had become unstoppable. Popular hatred of Israel, which Nasser did nothing to discourage, now swept him forward and drove other Arab leaders to his side. Even King Hussein of Jordon, for years at odds with Nasser, decided that he could no longer stand aloof. King Hussein, Jordon, "That morning I got into my aircraft and made the journey to Cairo, and I was met by the president. I was in military fatigues with my gun on, and they said, 'Well, I see you are carrying a gun,' and I said, 'I have been like that for the last couple of days with my troops.' And then he made a strange remark. 'What would happen if we took you prisoner and denied all knowledge of you arriving in this country?'"

Soon after, King Hussein signed a mutual defense treaty with Nasser and agreed to put his army under Egyptian command.

(May 30, 1967) Hussein, "We were on the verge of a war. Therefore, any reservations I had, in the past, of any troops coming into Jordon were removed as far as I was concerned."

So Israel faced the prospect of war on three fronts—from Jordon in the east, from Syria in the north, and from Egypt in the south.

General Narkiss, Israeli commander, "That was the time when Auschwitz came up. It had never happened before. When people spoke, they said there was a feeling, 'We are surrounded, we are surrounded. No one will help us. No one is helping us.' And God forbid if the Arab armies invade us, they will kill us all."

By this point, Israel had been mobilized for more than two weeks. All males age eighteen to fifty-five were called to serve. Most vehicles were requisitioned. Most factories closed. Israel could not stay fully mobilized for long. But still Prime Minister Eshkol waited for the International community to do something. He came to military headquarters to remind his generals of America's warning. "Israel must not go it alone."

General Gavish, Israeli Commander, "He told us that they were making diplomatic efforts in the United States and Europe. They were trying to reach a deal with Nasser. It made no sense to us."

Flanked by Rabin, Eshkol found himself surrounded by generals insisting on a preempted strike. General Pelit was usually very quiet. Now, he was shouting. He was actually shrieking. "Why do you hesitate? Why are you afraid?"

General Weizman, Head of Organizations, Israel, "I said, 'Eshkol, you have the best army since King David. If you do not attack, you will never be forgiven. If you do, you will be the conquering hero.'"

To regain the confidence of his generals, Prime Minister Eshkol appointed a new prime minister of defense, the hero of the 1956 Suez War, Mosha Dian.

June 1, 1967, Dian, "Although their numbers and forces are greater and bigger than ours, I am hoping that we can make it, but much depends on where the battles are." The generals also asked for another envoy to be sent to Washington. The prime minister agreed.

General Meir Amit, Head of Mossad, Israel, "He said, 'Listen, Meir. You go to Washington and find out what's going on there. Are the Americans organizing a naval task force? Is anybody going to do anything? When?'" Amit's mission was to see if the Americans planned to open the Straights of Tehran or if Israel would have to act alone.

Walt Rostow, National Security Advisor, United States: "The Pentagon had quite enough trouble in Vietnam, and didn't want another war. The director of the CIA made it perfectly clear. There is no international naval force. There are no American plans for action. There is no task force."

So the head of the Mossad, Israeli Intelligence Agency, called on the department of defense.

Amit, "You know our situation. I am here on the instruction of my prime minister."

Rostow, "He was doing most of the talking. I did ask one or two questions."

Amit, "At the meeting, I realized that America, because of Vietnam, was unwilling to act alone and that they did not succeed in organizing the international naval force. Also, Eisenhower made a commitment to Israel about the Straights in 1956, so America would no longer oppose Israel acting on its own."

Robert McNamara, Defense Secretary, United States, "I was friendly during my discussion and friendly as he left, but uh, he didn't ask for answers and he got no answers."

Amit raced back to Israel, the cabinet and the prime minister not to expect any international help. Amit, "I gave a detailed account of my trip to Washington, and I said I recommend we launch the war as soon as possible, not one of the ministers disagreed."

Miriam Eshkol, Israeli prime minister's wife, "We went for our usual walk. Suddenly, he (Eshkol) starts humming. He was totally tone deaf. He had this Hasidic song he liked to sing. He sang it over and over again."

Eshkol, "The rabbi has told us to enjoy ourselves because hard times are coming."

Miriam Eshkol, "So I asked him, 'What's happened dearest?' And he told me, tomorrow the war will start. There will be widows. There will be orphans. There will be bereaved parents. Who knows what tomorrow will bring.'"

The generals chose the morning of June 5 for the attack. General Hod, Commander, Israeli Air Force, "The commander in chief and I took a decision. On the night of June 4, we would sleep at home. The tom-toms in Israel work like in the jungle. If the chief of staff and the air force chief both come home, word gets around that tomorrow is going to be quiet. That was the Commanders bedtime message." Leaving behind only 12 fighters to defend Israel, 180 aircraft took off for Egypt. Their target was forty-five minutes away.

Ran Peker, Israeli squadron leader, "We observed total radio silence. We flew at the height of the waves for about fifteen minutes. We flew low over the sand dunes. We crossed the Suez Canal at Kantara and entered the Delta. As we flew over the Delta, farmers waved at us. They probably thought we were Egyptians." Most of the Israeli squadrons flew out into the sea far to west. They had extra fuel tanks to enable them to approach Egypt's air bases from an unexpected direction.

Peker, "That was the longest forty-five minutes of my life. The hands on my watch didn't seem to move. They went very slowly."

As the Israeli bombers approached their targets, the Egyptians received a coded message from Jordan. General Noufal, Deputy Chief of Operations, Egypt, "They spotted Israeli plans heading toward us, so they sent us a signal from their radar base to warn us. The signal was in code. Our codes had changed the day before and we had real trouble decoding it."

General Fawzi, chief of staff, Egypt, "The Ministry of Defense asked the air defense people what they had done with the signal they had received. It had the code word 'grape.' They replied, 'What signal.'"

Peker, "At exactly 0745, we pulled up to six thousand feet. I looked down and saw the MiG glinting at the edges of the runway. I could see the pilots sitting in the cockpits. I knew we had caught them by surprise."

The Israelis started the attack by destroying the runways to prevent the Egyptians from taking off. The few that did get off the ground were no match for the Israeli fighters.

General Noufal, "I got a call from one of the Air Force Chiefs. He said, 'Noufal, Noufal!'"

"I said, 'Yes, sir?'"

"He said, 'Our air fields are being attacked'"

"I said, 'What the hell are you talking about?'"

"He said, 'Our air fields are being attacked.'"

"I said, 'Our air fields?'"

"He said, 'The air fields in the Sinai are being attacked.'"

"I said, 'All the Sinai air fields? Tell me it's not true.'"

"He said, 'Believe me, all the air fields are being attacked.'"

"I hung up. The phone rang again. It was another commander. He said, 'We are being attacked.'"

"So I said to myself, 'Well, something must be going on,' but I was all alone."

He was alone because the head of the Egyptian Armed Forces, Amir, had left with the Minister of War and his top brass to inspect his positions in the Sinai.

Shams Badran, Minister of War, Egypt, "Ten minutes after takeoff, we heard about the Israeli attack. We turned around and flew back. Our cars had gone. We had to hail a taxi to get back to headquarters." By the time Amir's taxi got him back to headquarters, Egypt's Air Force was destroyed.

Noufal, "Amir was panicking. He told the Air Force Chief to implement the counterattack plan. The Air Force Chief replied, 'How can 1.1 have no aircraft.'" In the Sinai, Egypt had three times as many tanks as Israel, but with no air cover, their situation was dire.

Noufal, "Amir told me, 'Draw up a plan of retreat. Bring the troops back across the Canal.' Marshall Amir had been a close friend of President Nasser for more than twenty years. They had fought together as young officers. Together they had planned the coup which brought down the Egyptian monarchy. Now, the president phoned his defeated Army commander. I was the only other person there. Amir was in tears. He was calling Nasser by his first name. He said, 'Let me bring our boys back safely.' When he put the phone down, I asked 'Why are you crying?' He said, 'Nasser had said, "Forgive me, I have caused this catastrophe."' Nasser had been crying too."

Marshall Amir did not wait for his chief of staff to plan a retreat. He simply picked up the phone and gave the order himself.

Noufal, "The order was 'Withdraw back. Leave the artillery behind.'" Amir's order was a disaster. His retreating units could not protect each other. The Israelis gave chase.

General Gavish, Israeli commander, "Our tanks had Egyptian tanks in front and behind them. We attacked them from the ground and the air. Thousands were destroyed. It was a terrible sight." 338 Israelis were killed, but the Egyptian dead numbered fifteen thousand.

Days earlier when the war had begun, the Israelis had contacted the king of Jordan. General Weizman, Head of Operations, Israel, "We did not plan to take Jerusalem or the West Bank. We did not plan to take the Golan. On the fifth, we sent a telegram to the Americans, to King Hussein, that the war was between us and the Egyptians. If Jordan stayed out, nothing would happen. But at about ten thirty, he started shelling Jerusalem."

June 5, 1967, Jerusalem

General Narkiss, Israeli commander, Jordanian front, "Teddy Kolak, the major of Jerusalem, asked me at the command post what he should do with the children in the kindergartens and schools. In the command post, we looked at each other. We said, 'This is not nice. We'll take on Hussien.' The deputy chief of staff called me. He said, 'Uzi, you are authorized to enter the old city. You will have to be quick and use your head.'"

It took the Israelis ten hours of bitter street fighting to defeat the Jordan legion street fighters, to defeat the old city. Once the troops had broken through to the Wailing Wall, keeping the city united under Israel's rule became the basic role of the government.

When the battle ended, Jordan had lost not only the old city, but all of the land of the West Bank of the Jordan River.

King Hussein, Jordan, "When I went out and I could see people crossing over in small groups, very tired. Through all the years that I have spent since 1953 since, I have tried to build the country and build that army; on the roads . . . I saw it just destroyed. I never received a more crushing blow than that."

June 7, 1967

"Mr. Prime Minister, does Israel wish any territory beyond the territory she already holds?"

Levi Eshkol, "No sir, no sir! We don't need any additional territory. We want to dwell on this territory that we already have. There is so much to put in, money, energy, brains and ah we don't want any additional territory."

With Jordan and Egypt defeated, Israel turned its might on the Golan Heights, the site of frequent attacks from Syria.

General Meir Amit, Head of Mossad, Israel, "Dian said, 'We are going to take the Golan now.' I remember that some members of the religious parties were opposed to this. Dian was adamant. He said, 'We're not going to lose time. I've delayed it this long because we wanted to finish with the Egyptians and the Jordanians.'"

Hod, "We threw everything we had at the Golan Heights. In twelve hours, we dropped more bombs on the Golan than we had on all of the Egyptian airfield—rockets, bombs, napalm . . . everything we had."

The whole war had been sparked by a false Soviet report of a threat to Syria. Now that Israel was actually attacking Syria, the Soviets were forced to react. Walt Rostow, National Security Advisor, United States, "Word came through the hotline. I didn't know what it was about because I thought the war was pretty much over. Nevertheless, I went right back immediately to the White House, the usual suspects were there, McNamara was there and the rest. We had a very hairy message from the Russians."

June 10, 1967, McNamara, "The Soviets made it very clear that they would intervene militarily, and very likely, they would not only turn Israel back from its attack on Syria, but they would join Syria in an effort to deal a mortal blow to Israel. It was a very, very dangerous situation." The Soviets did not seem to be bluffing. Strategic bomber command in the Ukraine had received orders to prepare four squadrons to fly to the battle zone.

General Reshetnikov, Soviet Bomber Command, "It was all arraigned in a great hurry. We were given strict instructions not to suffer any casualties. The loss of even one Soviet airplane would betray our involvement. But we saw this as unrealistic, so we had to find another way." The pilots were then ordered to leave behind all identification. Their planes were to be repainted in Egyptian colors. "I ordered red stars. Our only one color red. But it turned out we needed four different colors. I remember green and black, and something else, maybe red, but we didn't have the right colors, so that caused a lot of fuss."

In the White House situation room, President Johnson and his staff worked out his response to the Soviet ultimatum. The president sent a message over the hotline telling the Kremlin that he was using every means to get Israel to stop the war. This was not strictly true, although he could've phoned the Israeli prime minister directly, he phoned the Israeli ambassador at the UN instead.

Gideon Rafael, Israeli ambassador to the UN, "United States Ambassador Gorvec asked me to come out into the lobby, and he said to me, 'You must immediately announce that the fighting is over.'" This was not within the Israeli ambassador's power so he asked his boss, Abba Eban, to phone the prime minister, but Eshkol was with his generals on the Golan Heights.

Miriam Eshkol, Israeli prime minister's wife, "Suddenly, Eban calls and says, 'Tell Eshkol to stop the war. We are under terrible pressure here at the UN' Then, Eshkol calls me and he says, 'Aw, this Golan is absolutely fantastic! The view is wonderful.'

"And I tell him, 'Eshkol, Eban wants you to stop the war. He can't take the pressure.'

"He said, 'I can't hear you.'

"What do you mean you can't hear me. I am telling you in Eban's exact words.

"He says, 'I can't hear you. I can't hear you. It's a bad line. It's a bad line. I'll come home and then we'll talk.' And then I understood. They wanted time to conquer more kilometers."

The Israelis pressed on into the Golan and encountered no Soviet forces because President Johnson had raised the stakes. He asked McNamara, "What distance from the Syrian coast the American fleet was at the time?"

"And he said, 'One hundred miles. It was steaming toward Gibraltar on a training exercise. We turned it around.'"

"And the president said, 'Move them to within fifty miles,'" knowing that the fleet was shadowed by Soviet electronic ships and that they would know it directly. That was also part of the message.

General Reshetnikov, Soviet Bomber Command, "So our secret invasion by the back door never happened. Thank God for that." The Israeli government waited until their forces had achieved their objective before ordering them to halt.

Eban, "A text of an agreed statement of cease-fire was given. I read this statement, slowly translating it from Hebrew to English and that was the end of the war."

In six days, the armed forces had quadrupled the territory Israel controlled. From Syria they had taken the Golan Heights; from Jordon, the West Bank and the old city of Jerusalem; from Egypt, the Gaza and the Sinai. With so much new territory to trade, Israel had its best chance for peace. Israelis flocked to the old city. To them, the victory was a deliverance from destruction. The Israeli cabinet was determined to hold onto Jerusalem, the West Bank, but in exchange for peace, they were willing to give the Golan Heights back to Syria and the Sinai to Egypt. The foreign minister told the Americans of Israelis' offer. Abba Eban, foreign minister, Israel, "When I presented these in a meeting that included Rusk Dolberg and Sisco in general, they were astonished by the fact that we were clearly not in the mood of annexation."

Joseph Sisco, U.S. delegate to the UN, "That, we believed then, a rather remarkable initiative on the part of the Israelis because we were operating on the assumption, Eban had told us some days before; 'we are not interested in territory.'"

That week, President Johnson was hosting a summit for Soviet Prime Minister Kosegan. Eager to appear as peace makers at the UN, the two leaders had a peace resolution drafted. In Cairo, it was scrutinized by the Foreign Ministry. This was another turning point in the Arab/Israeli conflict.

Salah Bassiouny, Foreign Ministry, Egypt, "We concluded that this proposal was the best we were likely to get. We advised the foreign minister to accept it." The minister looked at it differently.

Anatoly Dobrynin, Soviet ambassador to the United States, "When the resolution was proposed, Israel was ready to accept it, but Egypt's prime minister was totally against the resolution because it indirectly implied Israel's right to exist, and he wouldn't have that at all. Israel of course did not want any resolution that only said pull back your forces but didn't recognize Israel's existence, so this was the problem." But recognizing Israel was not on Nasser's agenda. Following Egypt's defeat, he had more immediate problems at home.

General Fawzi, chief of staff, Egypt, "Abdul Nasser said, 'We have lost. There is no point in staying on. I shall resign.'"

June 9, 1967

Nasser, Cairo, "I have decided to resign totally and finally from all official positions. I shall return to private life. I shall perform my duties like any other citizen."

After his broadcast, crowds surrounded the presidential palace and begged Nasser to stay. Shams Badran, Minister of War, Egypt, "Most of the demonstrations were genuine. Most of the people were upset. But something else happens to. The party boss told everyone to gather and listen to the speech. After the speech, they took to the streets and chanted, 'We want Nasser. No one but Nasser!'" Nasser stayed on as president. His old friend Marshall Amir became his scapegoat. He refused to resign and Nasser had him arrested. He died in custody. It was said in Cairo, it was suicide. Shortly after, Nasser rejected the Soviet/American peace plan. Nasser could not bring himself to accept the peace plan. He was a hero to the Arabs. He couldn't be seen negotiating with the Israelis.

September 1967, Khartoum, Sudan

Three months later, Arab leaders met to formulate a unified policy against Israel. Nasser, still the idol of the Arab world was subdued.

King Hussein, "I thought different man. I noticed from the outset that he felt a great deal of guilt."

The Arabs agreed to reject any compromise from Israel.

Zeid Rifa'I, Head of Royal Court, Jordan, "The decision of the Arab countries not to negotiate with Israel, not to make peace with Israel, and not to recognize Israel."

With no recognition of Israel, no negotiation, and no peace, it was only a matter of time before war would break out again.

Palestinian Exiles 1970-1982

At the Suez Canal, now the border between Egypt and Israel, the Egyptians launched a war of attrition, and the Israelis fought back. With growing casualties, political attitudes in both countries hardened. There was growing conflict in the Jordan Valley as well. Israeli soldiers were in constant pursuit of Palestinians who crossed into the West Bank to attack Israeli targets. There was no talk of peace. Inside Jordan, the Palestinians were busy building up their forces. Their charter called for the replacement of Israel by a Palestine state and the expulsion of all Jews who arrived after

1948. In 1967, a small band of Palestinian guerillas set up a camp in Karami, in the Jordan River valley. From the bank of the Jordan, they could see the Israeli soldiers patrolling the West Bank.

Abu Ali Shaheen, Palestinian fighter, "We waited until the Israeli patrol vehicle had passed by. Then, we started to cross the river. The first to cross was Abu Amar." Abu Amar, or Yasser Arafat, was an engineer who became one of the founders of a resistance group called Fatah. This was their first crossing of the river Jordan, launching their campaign to establish a Palestinian State.

Yasser Arafat, Fatah leader, "We knew it would not be easy, but we are ready to pay the price."

Shaheen, "On me, the water of the river came up to here (his neck). On taller people, of course it wouldn't come so far up. Now, Arafat is short and the water came up to his shoulders. He had his clothes on top of his head and he wadded slowly, slowly. If he slipped, he would fall and everything would get wet, especially his gun."

Beyond the river in the occupied West Bank, the Fatah guerillas set about recruiting and training small resistance groups to strike at Israel. "The best targets were the ones we could take by surprise, for example, moving vehicles. You open fire. A group of three or four of you, then if you throw one or two grenades, that settles it. You are safe and they are dead."

The guerillas had the support of Jordan's regular army. General Haditha, Jordanian Army, "At first, I encouraged them when they went on operations. We would provide covering fire as they crossed the river. If the Israelis hit back, the kingdom of Jordan would take the blow. So I asked His Majesty to meet them."

King Hussein, "I had never seen a photograph of Arafat, just had a description of him. So I was looking at a big burly figure that I thought must be Arafat, but when he finally came to say good-bye, I suddenly realized it wasn't." The actions launched from Kamari worried the king, but he was unable to stop them.

General Tal, Israeli commander, "Karami had become a huge military base in Jordan. The terrorists there were sending units into Israel. The straw that broke the camel's back was an attack on an Israeli bus taking pupils on a school trip south of the Dead Sea. It hit a Palestinian mine. Children were killed and injured." In response, the Israeli army was ordered to destroy the Palestinian bases in Karami and South of the Dead Sea.

General Narkiss, Israeli commander, "We were not very careful. After the 1967 war, we did not take the enemy seriously. We didn't bother to hide any of our troop movements."

King Hussein, Jordan, "They came blatantly with tanks, artillery, troops. So we realize that something was about to happen. I think they were overconfident."

March 21, 1968

King Hussein, Jordan, "And at about five in the morning, we were told that they had crossed one of the bridges. The Israelis attacked, facing them, with three hundred Palestinian fighters with orders from Arafat to hold their ground. By midday, half of them were dead and most of the rest had been rounded up. Arafat had slipped out of there at two o'clock in the morning, but the battle wasn't over yet. Jordanian army tanks arrived in force. I jumped when I was told the Israeli tanks were coming. I jumped out of bed. 'Shoot,' I said. I was jumping with excitement. I wanted to face the Jews. I wanted to teach them a lesson. Yes, by God, I did. The Jordanian involvement in the battle was very massive. We destroyed many of their tanks." Twenty-nine Israelis died in the battle. The Palestinians declared victory.

Yasser Arafat, Fatah leader "We faced these huge up-to-dates on the victory over Israeli forces. In the beginning, we were alone. After five hours, some smaller battalions from the Jordanian government attended us and fought with us without any central instructions from their government, but ah, it was the first victory for the Arab Nation after the big defeat in 1967."

King Hussein, "They claimed it to be a victory for them, ah, we wouldn't have disputed that except for the fact that it wasn't true."

But it was a public relations triumph. Arafat was chosen to command all the factions in the Palestine Liberation Organization. Inspired by stories of a great victory at Kirami, volunteers from many countries came to swell the ranks.

General Haditha, Jordanian Army, "But unfortunately, the majority were the worst type of people, they were untrained and undisciplined. The PLO grew larger and our problems grew with it."

Zeid Rifa'l, Head of Royal Court, Jordan, "Instead of anarchy, we had fifty-two different guerilla organizations of all various types, and they weren't just Palestinian organizations. Every international guerilla organization had a presence in the country."

Yasser Abed Rabbo, Democratic Front for the Liberation of Palestine, "We were naive people. We were very enthusiastic, very revolutionary. At the same time, we were, I can reassure you, we were very innocent. We felt that King Hussein as a reactionary leader leading a reactionary regime as an obstacle and in order to make our revolution succeed, we need to remove this obstacle."

One day, shooting broke out in the Capital, Aman and the king drove out to investigate. King Hussein, Jordan, "And at across the road, where there was military check posts, we found that one side of the road was closed and the other side was blocked by a bloody body. As we came to a stop, suddenly, we were under very intense, heavy machine gun fire. The guard car in front of me was hit. We lost a Sergeant of my guard and about four wounded. Everyone jumped out of my car and yelled at me to do the same. We could see the bullets from the semi-machine guns coming down at us, hitting the asphalt, the tar around us. It was like raindrops on a parched land, just making holes, and ah, those holes were getting closer and closer to where we were standing."

Hussein, "I got very angry, and I said, 'How dare they?'" The king jumped into a ditch.

Aman, "Spontaneously, on the spur of the moment, I had an idea to protect His Majesty physically and the Commander of the Guards had the idea at the same time."

King Hussein, "They both came after me at the same time to give me body cover and nearly broke my back in the process." Their driver turned the car around.

Hussein, "We got into the car, shooting going on, engine was revving like mad, but we were still stationary, and I told the driver to hold on a second. Let's put it in gear, in his moment of anxiety he had forgotten to do, and in a second, we drove off."

The faction most determined to overthrow the government of Jordan was led by George Habash. Dr. George Habash, Popular Front for the Liberation of Palestine, "All we wanted to do was to fight against Israel. But the Jordanian regime saw us as a danger and/or threat. This was their problem, not ours."

Yassir Arafat, PLO Chairman: "Dr. Habash who was the leader of a political party, and they decided to remove King Hussein. Not from our point of view. We don't like to fight against the government, but if they are insisting to clash, we fight."

On September 9, 1970, this British airliner with 115 passengers and some of Dr. Habash's armed men aboard appeared over Aman. Hussein: "I heard about it when an aircraft passed over my house in the city, and ah, the suburbs, and practically knocking the roof off."

In a singular, spectacular operation, Habash's men hijacked four Western airliners and forced three of them to fly to Jordan with their hundreds of passengers. The planes landed on an old WW II airstrip in the desert.

Nasser, "We waited for twenty full years. Nothing has happened. Our people remain in their camps, in their tents. They are fed up with this condition."

Habash, "We thought that the way to attract the world's attention to our cause was to hijack planes."

The Jordanian army surrounded the airstrip and the general in charge went in to negotiate with the hijackers.

General Haditha, Deputy in Chief of Armed Forces, Jordan, "We spoke for hours. It was terribly hot. I stayed in the shade of the aircraft. I made a deal with them. We take the passengers, they take the planes. 435 passengers and crew were taken off the aircrafts, but some were kept as hostages."

King Hussein, "The humiliation of having the aircraft flown into the country and innocent passengers being whisked away and being unable to do anything about it was something that questioned whether Jordan really existed." The hijackers then drove their message to the world. (They blew up some of the planes) Hussein, "Well, that was really it as far as I was concerned. Something had to be done and done soon."

September 16, 1970

Four days later with control of the kingdom slipping away, King Hussein declared war on the PLO. That day, Jordanian tanks and soldiers moved into position around the capital. Arab was poised to fight Arab. He said, "I think I tried to get a little bit sleep that night. I prayed a lot. In the morning, at first light, there was movement into the city. On the early hours of September 17, I woke up when we had the artillery bombing our bases."

Yasser Abed Rabbo, Democratic Front for the Liberation of Palestine, "So what we did immediately, we went to Arafat's office, the joint command. Arafat was there. That was where most of the leaders were there, Habash was there, and they were calling to telephone wireless Damascus and telling them about the loss and asking them in an open way for Syrian intervention." On the third day of fierce fighting, the Syrians responded.

Prince Bin Shakir, Jordan Army, "Our intelligence and our radar informed us that civilians were massing tank formations on the Jordanian/Syrian border."

King Hussein, "We had been arguing over this invasion, particularly with our Soviet friends at the time. Whenever I raised the problem with the Soviet ambassador, he would respond but these are Palestinian army units and Palestinian army tanks, not Syrian."

Shakir, "And we all knew that the PLO does not have tanks." But there were tanks. Soviet built ones streaming in from Syria.

General Tlas, deputy defense minister, Syria, "We were just protecting the Palestinians from the army of Jordan. Our purpose wasn't really to attack the Jordanians. It was a limited intervention on the smallest possible scale. All we wanted to do was support and protect the Palestinian fighters." In Washington, President Nixon called in his National Security Advisors to assess the reports from Jordan. Alexander Haig, Deputy National Security Advisor, United States, "The Soviets were on every platoon leader's tank right up to the border and then jumped off as they crossed the border, then Syrian officers were in command of what were allegedly PLO volunteer forces, so we knew immediately it was an international crisis." The president summoned the Soviet ambassador.

President Richard Nixon, Interviewed by David Frost, 1977, "We warned the Russians—stay out of there. They of course in turn warned us and said, 'You stay out and keep Israel out.'"

In the meantime, King Hussein's forces had destroyed many of the Syrian tanks, but they could not stop the advance. The pressure on the king was increasing by the hour.

Dean Brown, U.S. ambassador to Jordan, "When the Syrian tanks had reached Irbit, which is about two-thirds of the way from the Syrian border down to Aman, right about that town, right on the edge of it. That's when he was really starting to panic."

King Hussein, "With all the threats from every direction, and for all intensive purposes looking impossible to comprehend, my headquarters started to tell me that we needed help from outside and that we should ask for it from the Americans and any quarter that would be willing to help." In these circumstances, any quarter could mean one thing—Israel.

Henry Kissinger, National Security Advisor, United States, "We knew that he would accept help from anyone, and we thought he would probably prefer direct American intervention."

Joseph Sisco, State Department, United States, "He was keenly aware that if he was resurrected and protected as a direct result of Israeli military intervention, that this would have a strongly negative impact not only within Jordan itself but obviously within the entire Arab world."

Kissinger, "This was something that was discussed between Sisco, myself, Haugue, and one or two of my staff people." The advisors knew that President Nixon would have to be informed about the situation right away. Kissinger, "At first I had to find him and the Secret Service told me he was in the basement of the Executive Office Building across the street from the White House, bowling, and that's where I found him. 'I remember Henry coming back into the office and saying holy mackerel, the guy's bowling with his black dress shoes on.' He was bowling alone. We just started talking. He wanted to have an American intervention there."

President Nixon, "And of course we just didn't have an empty cannon in there. That's why we moved complete units over into that part of the Mediterranean and that is why we alerted a couple of marine battalions as well."

Kissinger, "I thought it would be very difficult to manage if we didn't have a commander, we didn't have the right combination offerees, we didn't know how to end it."

Sisco, "Mr. President, we said, 'we think the Israelis are in the best position to do this. They are close to the scene. Their resources can be employed rapidly.'"

Kissinger, "Once he understood that he agreed to back the Israelis."

Nixon, "Hussein was quite aware of and approved of what we were doing in this thing, and if he didn't, he didn't let us know."

It was America's ambassador to Jordan who broke the news to King Hussein.

Dean Brown, U.S. ambassador to Jordan, "What I was told to say to him is we'll get the Israelis to come in and help you. And I think this is a very serious moment for the king."

Sisco, "We asked Rabin what the views of the Israeli government would be under these circumstance, and Rabin said he would report home and ask."

General Hood, commander, Israeli Air Force, "I got the authorization to send Phantoms to fly over these tanks. I briefed the leader of this formation myself. I told him, 'Fly over them. Make sure they see you and hear you. Make mock attacks so they understand what we want them to do. Go back.' So our four aircraft performed maneuvers over these tanks. On the side, I had another two quartets waiting just in case, but no one bothered them. They turned their tanks around and went back. A quartet of Phantoms was enough."

Whether it was because of Arab's solidarity or the threat of Nixon's sixth fleet and the threat of Israeli warplanes, Syria finally withdrew its tanks. The Jordanian army could now give all its attentions on kicking out the Palestinians. Yasser Arafat, hiding somewhere in the capital, sent out an SOS. Yasser Abed Rabbo, Democratic Front for the Liberation of Palestine, "I remember he made a broadcast through the station we had, asking the Arab world and the extending world to intervene." The Arab world heard him. It's leaders gathered in Cairo for an emergency meeting chaired by President Nasser. Nasser decided its leaders should send a delegation to Jordan to ask King Hussein to stop killing Palestinians. At the head of this delegation was the president of Sudan.

President Nimeiry, Sudan, "We went to King Hussein. Of course, he offered us every kind of delicious dish."

Hussein, "They kept telling us that you have to stop things immediately. Well, we can't stop. We are in the middle of a life and death struggle."

Nimeiry, "Then we stayed for dinner, going through all the arguments."

Hussein, "I believe that that experience was one my worst in that particular period of time because one is sad. One is worried. One is trying to deal with all kinds of problems every minute, and you try to entertain a group that is totally out of touch with the reality of the needs of the moment."

Nimeiry, "And we kept on talking and going through all the reasons until daybreak."

The Arab leaders, having failed to convince the king got into an armored car and turned on the radio. Nimeiry, "We started to hear Arafat talking and Arafat calling for help." The leaders went to Arafat's hideout and provided him with a new identity, a family man complete with wife and child. Nimeiry, "We passed off the child as Arafat's."

Chapter 12

The Five Basics

It seems every issue gets unnecessarily complicated. When it comes down to the Israel/Palestine conflict; there are only five basic issues. When you understand those five issues, you've got it. All the rest is merely a fill-in. The five basic issues are:

1. The right of return of the refugees
2. Borders
3. Settlements
4. Water rights
5. The Occupation

Let's look at issues one at a time

The Right of Return of the Refugees

When Modern Israel emerged in 1948, they put forth a huge effort for the right of return for their people. The brought-in plane loads of dark-skinned Ethiopian people only requiring if they could trace back to their heritage, no matter how many thousands of years ago; if they could show they had one drop of Hebrew blood anywhere in their ancestry, they were welcome. Plane loads of Ethiopians arrived. I know because I was there and saw hundreds of little children in indoctrination centers. Many of them have grown up, and today, when you go to Israel, you will see Ethiopian soldiers in Israel uniform. There is nothing confusing about it. It's a simple fact of life there.

In the past negotiation with the Palestinians, the issue of rights of return for the Palestinian refugees (one and a half million are in Jordan this day) was not on the table. It cannot be discussed. Some say it is because Israel believes it would, in time, tilt the balance of the population in favor of the Palestinians.

It seems so obvious, that if the Palestinians are not allowed the right of return, there can be no peace. It's like sixty years of displacement for nothing. Is Israel saying: "Yes, we will have peace with you, but none of the Palestinians can ever return?" Israel can have peace and allow the Palestinians the right of return. What is Israel afraid of? Is the real issue that they fear an imbalance of population in favor of Palestine? And if Israel really wants to be considered a democracy to the rest of the world that one vote for each person will in time tilt to Palestine and Palestine will eventually become the majority population. Why does Israel always insist that there will never be a right of return for the Palestinians? The notion that this will eventually wind up in tilting the population in favor of the Palestinians can easily be cured. One way is simply to phase in the migration into Israel. That is to say allow 10-15 percent to migrate annually or any of a dozen formulas that will accomplish the right of return of the Palestinians without tilting the balance toward the Palestinians. In some areas, the current ratio is eighteen to one.

The bottom line is that this is not insurmountable, and it can be achieved.

Borders

The United Nations Partition Plan basically divided the land fifty-fifty (Not quite; it was 51 percent Israel, 49 percent Palestine, but let's not argue over 2 percent.)

In 1948, when Israel first invaded Palestine, they captured the land given to them by the UN Partition Plan. (The Green Line) However, they didn't stop there. With a superior army (mostly funded by U.S. taxpayer dollars), their military which consisted of the Stern Gang, the Irgun (a known terrorist organization) and the Palmauch went past the Green Line and continued to capture land that was given to Palestine.

I can understand the military going to their line and even defending it. When they went over the line, they were in violation of the UN Partition Plan and International law.

By the end of 1948, Israel had control of 72 percent of the land. This led to fighting for almost the next twenty years. This led to the 1967 war, which Israel won decisively. They did not stop there; they went on to capture even more land. Today Israel has control of more than 90 percent of the land and continuing to get more.

Today (actually for many years now), Palestine has conceded to the 72 percent Israel had control in 1967.

Palestine today is asking (demanding) Israel to go back to the 1967 borders. In essence, Palestine is saying: "OK, you win. We concede. You get the 72 percent, we get the remaining 23 percent." Palestine will not budge off this figure and the International community is with Palestine on this issue. Is ninety to ten fair? No. Is seventy-two to twenty-three fair? No, but Palestine is willing to concede to the pre-1967 borders. Palestine will settle for 23 percent. Nothing less. Palestine will never settle for anything less than the 23 percent. If Israel is serious about Peace, then they must concede every piece of land they have illegally confiscated over the 73 percent. Israel gets 73 percent, and Palestine concedes and accepts the 23 percent. It isn't fair to the Palestinians, but in the name of peace, they are willing to concede to the 1967 borders.

The sad thing about this issue is that every time it comes to the world's attention, Israel plays the victim and too many people buy into it. Most of the world's nations that are concerned about this issue are in agreement with Palestine. Of course, Israel isn't, and they put up a very powerful denial that would make an Eskimo believe he needs another refrigerator.

There have been many books written on this issue. (All five of the issues, actually) I'm trying to keep it simple. Too many pendants want to complicate the issues, which leads to too much misunderstanding and confusion. It ends up being a paralysis of analysis.

Settlements

Some people, when they hear the word "settlements" think of a tent city. This is not so in Modern Israel/Palestine.

Settlements are neighborhoods and villages and towns elaborately planned and built for people coming into Israel/Palestine to "settle." Some of them rival many expensive neighborhood developments built in America.

Israelis like to claim they are building "facts on the ground." The implication is, of course, once they are built and occupied by Jews, it will be very difficult (practically impossible) to move them out.

The problem is that they are illegal. They are built on illegally occupied land, and building houses on illegally occupied land is not only against local laws and national laws, it is in violation of International law.

The United Nations has declared the settlements are illegal and has demanded the land be returned to the Palestinians. Continuing to build them is both illegal and an obstacle to peace.

Perhaps, the most classic example of this is when Yitzhak Shamir was prime minister, he appealed to George Bush Sr. for a ten-billion-dollar (that's correct "Billion") loan guarantee for new settlements.

President Bush wouldn't agree because he claimed that settlements are an obstacle to peace. Of course, this enraged the American Jewish establishment. They turned against President Bush.

President Bush risked the Jewish vote and appealed to the American Public on national television. The American public rallied in favor of President Bush, and the request for the ten-billion-dollar loan guarantee was defeated. It cost Shamir the next election.

The Israelis are very cleaver, and they always have "Plan B." They appealed to President Bush and requested that since they couldn't get the loan guarantee, would he do them a "small" favor and request to the United Nation to rescind its declaration that Israel is a "Racist" country.

Within a few days, President Bush appeared in front of the United Nations on National Television and requested that the United Nations rescind their declaration that Israel is a racist country pleading that Modern Israel was a fledging country trying to establish democracy, and would the United Nations have compassion on them and rescind their declaration claiming Israel a racist country? The United Nations rescinded their claim.

It is important to point out that, even though the United Nations rescinded their declaration that Israel is a racist country, thirty thousand non-government organizations (NGO'S) at their following meeting continued to declare Israel a racist Country. So who is fooling whom? I shall let the reader decide.

The irony of this issue of a failed ten-billion-dollar loan guarantee request by Shamir is that Rabin persuaded the Israel government he could get the money, and he did.

He came to America, and on national network telecast, mimicked the famous Bush line: "Read my lips," saying: "Read my lips, no new settlements." Rabin got the ten-billion-dollar loan funds and won the election.

Pretty slick, huh? And the American public was mostly unaware because it didn't receive the broad coverage that President Bush received when he earlier appealed to them on national television to get the original request rescinded.

Of course, Rabin used the loan guarantees to continue building settlement. When Rabin was confronted by a journalist saying: "How is it that you said 'Read my lips, no new settlements.' You are building more settlements?"

Rabin's reply (A classic), "I said, '"No more new" settlements. We're not building "new" settlements. We're just "completing" settlements already approved.'"

As an American, does this make your blood boil? Do you feel you're being used? It's your tax dollars. You are footing the bill.

Water Rights

Simply speaking, Israel has illegally taken over all the water aquafiers and charge the Palestinians for water. Also, they often shut off the water supply as a means to punish the Palestinians. This must stop.

The Occupation

There's a popular slogan in the occupied territories; "its the occupation stupid." The occupation of East Jerusalem, the occupation of the West Bank, the occupation of Gaza. This is against the United Nations declarations, International Law, and the Fourth Geneva Convention. Books have been written on this subject. Need I say more?

Chapter 13

The Sabra Shatila Massacre

Since 1948, Israel has had a rather simple agenda; Israeli supremacy and power and to smear the Palestinians. Israel also has been very successful in covering up a lot of their violations of International Law. Israel doesn't want to bring world attention and condemnation to their misdeeds and have been incredibly clever in hiding many of them.

The Sabra Shatila Massacre put an end to all of that, once and for all. For the first time, in its brief history, Israel was finally caught! Who caught them? The Israeli public.

The news spread so fast, even though the Israeli government denied they had anything to do with and so did the IDF. It's their policy to deny everything, no matter how huge the evidence is against them. But this was too big. The Israel public demanded an investigation, going all the way to the Israeli Supreme Court. The pressure that the Israeli public put on their own government forced the Israeli Supreme Court to order an in-depth investigation into this atrocious incident.

What happened and who did it?

⟨⟩*Sabra and Shatila massacre*

1982—Sabra and Shatila—The number of deaths at these Palestinian refugee camps in Lebanon is disputed to be between 400 to upwards of 3,000, mostly civilians. This massacre drew international condemnation and the UN General Assembly termed it an act of genocide by a vote of 123-0 with 22 abstentions (the United States abstained). An outcry in Israel led to the establishment of an investigation led by Yitzhak Kahan, then President of the Israeli Supreme Court. The Kahan Commission found that Israel was indirectly responsible for the massacre and that Ariel Sharon (whose career continued unabated after the Qibya massacre) bore personal responsibility. The Kahan Commission recommended Sharon be dismissed from his post as defense minister and never hold a ministerial position again. After much debate, Sharon stepped down as defense minister but maintained a minister-without-portfolio position in the government. It was during these years that President Ronald Reagan drew the conclusion that Sharon was a "bad guy who seemingly looks forward to a war." Sharon would go on to be elected prime minister.

The *Sabra and Shátila massacre* (Arabic: مذبحة صبرا وشاتيلا *Maḏbaḥat Ṣabrā wa Shātīlā*)—or *Sabra and Chatila massacre*—was a massacre of Palestinian and Lebanese Muslim civilians carried out between 16 and 18 September 1982 by the Kataeb Party, a Christian Lebanese Forces militia group, following the assassination of Phalangist leader and president-elect Bachir Gemayel. The Israeli Defense Force (IDF), who surrounded Beirut's Palestinian refugee camps after having invaded Lebanon, allowed the Lebanese Forces militia to enter two of these refugee camps, Sabra and Shatila and continue the massacre throughout the night by shooting flares to illuminate the camp(⊕33°51'40.47"N 35°30'01.50"E / 33.8612417°N 35.500417°E). The exact number killed by the Lebanese Forces militia is disputed, with estimations running from 800 according to international sources to 3,500 according to Palestinian sources (the red cross body count was around 400, but is likely not to include all or even most of the dead bodies).

Regarded as a reprisal for the Damour massacre by Islamic Palestinians and Syrians a few years earlier, which personally impacted Elie Hobeika. The view of the Sabra and Shatila killing as a revenge for the Damour massacre was asserted by the prominent writer Samir Khalaf, by New York Times writer Thomas Friedman, and by author B. Gabriel who wrote that "Palestinian militiamen started the killings in 1976, long before the 1982 Sabra and Shatila massacres. Beit Mellat, Deir Achache, Damour." The Damour massacre, however, had been a response to the Karantina massacre, which had taken place earlier in 1976. In the Karantina massacre, Phalangists killed an estimated 1500 Muslims.

The Phalangists stood under the direct command of Elie Hobeika, who later became a long-serving Member of Parliament and, in the 1990s, a cabinet minister. The Israeli military's Chief of Staff was Lt. General Rafael Eitan, and Israel's Defence Minister was Ariel Sharon.

Debate continues today regarding Israeli responsibility for the massacre (see section 'Israeli role in the massacre'). In 1982, an independent commission chaired by Sean MacBride concluded that the Israeli authorities or forces were, directly or indirectly, involved. The Israeli government established the Kahan Commission to investigate, and in early 1983 it found Israel *indirectly responsible* for the event, and that Ariel Sharon bears *personal responsibility* for the massacre for allowing the Phalangists into the camps. The Israelis had been supplying the Phalangists with weapons and equipment, and had provided transportation of the Phalangists to the camps. The commission, which was not a judicial body which could recommend criminal charges, but an investigative body only, demanded that Sharon resign as head of the Defence Ministry. Sharon initially refused to resign, but after the death of an Israeli and the injury of ten other Israelis from a hand grenade thrown into a dispersing Peace Now rally, a compromise was reached where he resigned as Defense minister, but remained in the cabinet as Minister without portfolio. Sharon would later be elected Prime Minister of Israel.

⍰Background

From 1975 to 1990, groups in competing alliances with neighboring countries fought against each other in the Lebanese Civil War. Infighting and massacres between these groups claimed several thousands of victims; notable massacres in this period included the Syrian-backed Karantina Massacre (January 1976) by the Phalangists against Palestinian refugees, Damour massacre (January 1976) by the PLO against Maronites and the Tel al-Zaatar Massacre (August 1976) by Phalangists against Palestinian refugees. The total death toll in Lebanon for the whole civil war period was around 200,000-300,000 victims.

The Civil War saw many shifting alliances among the main players; the Lebanese Nationalists, led by the Christian Phalangist party and militia, were allied initially with Syria then with Israel, which provided them with arms and training to fight against the Palestine Liberation Organization (PLO); other factions were allied with Syria, Iran, and other states of the region. In addition, Israel had been training, arming, supplying, and uniforming the Christian-dominated South Lebanon Army (SLA), led by Saad Haddad, since 1978.

Sabra is the name of a poor neighborhood in the southern outskirts of West Beirut, which is adjacent to the Shatila UNRWA refugee camp set up for Arab refugees in 1949. Over the years the populations of the two areas became ever more mingled, and the loose terminology "Sabra and Shatila camps" has become usual. Their populations had been swelled by Palestinians and Lebanese Shiites from the south fleeing the wars.

The PLO had been attacking Israel from southern Lebanon, and Israel had been bombing PLO positions in southern Lebanon[11]. The attempted assassination of Israeli Ambassador Shlomo Argov in London on June 4, 1982 by Abu Nidal's organization became a casus belli for a full-scale Israeli invasion of Lebanon. On June 6,

Israel invaded Lebanon with 60,000 troops in an act condemned by the UN Security Council. Two months later, under a U.S.-sponsored cease-fire agreement signed in late August, the PLO agreed to leave Lebanon under international supervision, and Israel agreed not to advance further into Beirut.

On August 23, 1982, Bachir Gemayel, who was very popular among Maronites, was elected President of Lebanon by the National Assembly. Israel had relied on Gemayel and his forces as a counterbalance to the PLO, and ties between Israel and Maronite groups had grown stronger.

On September 1, the expulsion of the PLO fighters from Beirut was completed. Two days later, Israel deployed its armed forces around the refugee camps.

The Israeli Premier Menachem Begin met Gemayel in Nahariya and strongly urged him to sign a peace treaty with Israel. According to some sources, Begin also wanted the continuing presence of the SLA in southern Lebanon (Haddad supported peaceful relations with Israel) in order to control attacks and violence, and action from Gemayel to move on the PLO fighters which Israel believed remained a hidden threat in Lebanon. However, the Phalangists, who were previously united as reliable Israeli allies, were now split because of developing alliances with Syria, which remained militarily hostile to Israel. As such, Gemayel rejected signing a peace treaty with Israel and did not authorize operations to root out the remaining PLO militants.

On September 14, 1982, Gemayel was assassinated in a massive explosion which demolished his headquarters. Eventually, the culprit, Habib Tanious Shartouni, who confessed to the crime turned out to be a member of the Syrian Social Nationalist Party and an agent of Syrian intelligence. The Palestinian and Muslim leaders denied any connection.

Within hours of the assassination, Israeli Defense Minister Ariel Sharon, supported by Begin, decided to occupy West Beirut, informing only then Foreign Minister Yitzhak Shamir and not consulting the Israeli cabinet. The same night Sharon began preparations for entering the Sabra-Shatila refugee camps. Thus on September 15, the Israeli army reoccupied West Beirut. This Israeli action breached its agreement with the United States not to occupy West Beirut; the US had also given written guarantees that it would ensure the protection of the Muslims of West Beirut. Israel's occupation also violated its peace agreements with Muslim forces in Beirut and with Syria.

Events

Following the assassination of Lebanese Christian President Bashir Gemayel, tensions built as Phalangists called for revenge.

By noon of September 15, the Israeli Defence Force (IDF) had completely surrounded the Sabra-Shatila camps, and controlled all entrances and exits by the means of checkpoints. The IDF also occupied a number of multi-story buildings as observation posts. Amongst those was the seven-story Kuwaiti embassy which, according to TIME magazine, had "an unobstructed and panoramic view" of the camps. Hours later, IDF tanks began shelling the camps.

Ariel Sharon and Chief of Staff Rafael Eitan met with the Lebanese Phalangist militia units, inviting them to enter the Sabra and Shatila refugee camps and telling them the PLO fighters were responsible for the assassination of their leader Bashir Gemayel[22]. Under the Israeli plan, Israeli soldiers would control the perimeters of the refugee camps and provide logistical support while the Phalangists would enter the camps, find the PLO fighters and hand them over to Israeli forces. The meetings concluded at 3:00 p.m. September 16.

An hour later, 1,500 militiamen assembled at Beirut International Airport, then occupied by Israel. Under the command of Elie Hobeika, they began moving towards the camps in IDF supplied Jeeps, following Israeli guidance on how to enter the camps. The forces were mostly Phalangist, though there were some men from Saad Haddad's "Free Lebanon forces." According to Ariel Sharon, the Phalangists were given "harsh and clear" warnings about harming civilians.

The first unit of 150 Phalangists entered the camps at 6:00 p.m. A battle ensued that at times Palestinians claim involved lining up Palestinians for execution. During the night the Israeli forces fired illuminating flares over the camps. According to a Dutch nurse, the camp was as bright as "a sports stadium during a football game."

At 11:00 p.m. a report was sent to the IDF headquarters in East Beirut, reporting the killings of 300 people, including civilians. The report was forwarded to headquarters in Tel Aviv and Jerusalem, where it was seen by more than 20 senior Israeli officers.

Further reports of these killings followed through the night. Some of these reports were forwarded to the Israeli government in Jerusalem and were seen by a number of Israeli senior officials.

For the next 36 to 48 hours, the Phalangists massacred the inhabitants of Sabra and Shatila, while Israeli troops guarded the exits and allegedly continued to fire flares at night.

At one point, a militiaman's radioed question to his commander Hobeika about what to do with the women and children in the refugee camp was overheard by an Israeli officer, who heard Hobeika's reply: "This is the last time you're going to ask me a question like that; you know exactly what to do." Phalangist troops could be heard laughing in the background. The Israeli officer reported this to his superior, Brig. Gen. Amos Yaron, who warned Hobeika against hurting civilians but took no further action. Lt. Avi Grabowsky was cited by the Kahan Commission as having seen (on that Friday) the murder of five women and children, and gave a hearsay report of a battalion commander saying of this, "We know, it's not to our liking, and don't interfere." Israeli soldiers surrounding the camps turned back Palestinians fleeing the camps, as filmed by a Visnews cameraman.

Later in the afternoon, a meeting was held between the Israeli Chief of Staff and the Phalangist staff. On Friday morning, the Israelis surrounding the camps ordered the Phalange to halt their operation, concerned about reports of a massacre. According to the Kahan Commission's report (based on a Mossad agent's report), the Chief of Staff concluded that the Phalange should "continue action, mopping up the empty camps south of Fakahani until tomorrow at 5:00 a.m., at which time they must stop their action due to American pressure." He stated that he had "no feeling that something irregular had occurred or was about to occur in the camps." At this meeting, he also agreed to provide the militia with a tractor, supposedly to demolish buildings.

On Friday, September 17, while the camps still were sealed off, a few independent observers managed to enter. Among them were a Norwegian journalist and diplomat Gunnar Flakstad, who observed Phalangists during their cleanup operations, removing dead bodies from destroyed houses in the Shatila camp.

The Phalangists did not exit the camps at 5:00 a.m. on Saturday as ordered. They forced the remaining survivors to march out of the camps, to the stadium for interrogations; this went on for the entire day. The militia finally left the camps at 8:00 a.m. on September 18. The first foreign journalists allowed into the camps at 9:00 a.m. found hundreds of bodies scattered about the camp. The first official news of the massacre was broadcast around noon.

Number of victims

The number of victims of the massacre is disputed. There is general agreement that the exact numbers are very hard to pin down, due to the chaotic conditions during and after the massacre, burials and initial victim-counting, as well as the fact that it has been an extremely politically sensitive issue even to the present day. It is thought that at least a quarter of the victims were Lebanese, the rest Palestinians. Here follow the main estimates that have circulated, ordered by number of deaths:

- A letter from the head of the Red Cross delegation to the Lebanese Minister of Defense, cited in the Kahan Commission report as "exhibit 153," stated that Red Cross representatives had counted 328 bodies; but the Kahan Commission noted that "this figure, however, does not include all the bodies . . ."

- The Kahan Commission said that, according to "a document which reached us (exhibit 151), the total number of victims whose bodies were found from 18.9.82 to 30.9.82 is 460," stating further that this figure consists of "the dead counted by the Lebanese Red Cross, the International Red Cross, the Lebanese Civil Defense, the medical corps of the Lebanese army, and by relatives of the victims." Thirty-five women and children were among the dead according to this account.
- Israeli figures, based on IDF intelligence, cite a figure of 700-800. In the Kahan Commission's view, "this may well be the number most closely corresponding with reality."
- According to the BBC, "at least 800" Palestinians died.
- Bayan Nuwayhed al-Hout in her *Sabra and Shatila: September 1982* gives a minimum consisting of 1,300 named victims based on detailed comparison of 17 victim lists and other supporting evidence, and estimates an even higher total.
- Robert Fisk, one of the first journalists to visit the scene, quotes (without endorsing) unnamed Phalangist officers as saying "that 2,000 Palestinians-women as well as men-had been killed in Chatila." In a 2002 article in The Independent, Fisk speaks of "1700 civilians murdered." The Palestinian Red Crescent put the number killed at over 2,000.
- In his book published soon after the massacre, the Israeli journalist Amnon Kapeliouk of *Le Monde Diplomatique,* arrived at about 2,000 bodies disposed of after the massacre from official and Red Cross sources and "very roughly" estimated 1,000-1,500 other victims disposed of by the Phalangists themselves to a total of 3,000-3,500.

Media and public reactions

According to the British-American historian Bernard Lewis—not yet corroborated by other sources—the massacre received much attention from the world media, predominantly "demonizing

Israelis for allowing the attack," and Lewis noticed public protests against Israel and against Jews in Italy and France.

Bernard Lewis voiced displeasure with the media coverage and protesting Europeans, and argued that journalists and protesters responded overwhelmingly to the massacre because they were glad to have an opportunity to blame Jews.

Genocide status

On December 16, 1982, the United Nations General Assembly condemned the massacre and declared it to be an act of genocide. The voting record on section D of Resolution 37/123, which "resolves that the massacre was an act of genocide," was: yes: 123; no: 0; abstentions: 22; non-voting: 12. The abstentions were: Belgium, Denmark, France, Germany (Federal Republic), Iceland, Ireland, Italy, Luxembourg, Netherlands, Norway, Portugal, Sweden, United Kingdom, U.S., Canada, Australia, New Zealand, Israel, Ivory Coast, Papua New Guinea, Barbados, and Dominican Republic.

Disputes with U.N. verdict

While all delegates who took part in the debate acknowledged that a massacre had taken place, the claim that it was a genocide was disputed. The delegate for Canada stated: "The term genocide cannot, in our view, be applied to this particular inhuman act".

The delegate of Singapore—voting "yes"—added: "My delegation regrets the use of the term 'an act of genocide' . . . [as] the term 'genocide' is used to mean acts committed with intent to destroy, in whole or in part, a national, ethnic, racial or religious group" and "We also question whether the General Assembly has the competence to make such determination."

The United States commented that "While the criminality of the massacre was beyond question, it was a serious and reckless misuse of language to label this tragedy genocide as defined in the 1948 Convention . . ."

Such comments led William Schabas, director of the Irish Centre for Human Rights at the National University of Ireland, to state: "the term genocide . . . had obviously been chosen to embarrass Israel rather than out of any concern with legal precision"

Israeli role in the massacre

MacBride commission report

In 1982, an independent commission, the International Commission to enquire into reported violations of International Law by Israel during its invasion of the Lebanon, was formed. Chaired by Sean MacBride, the commission included the following members:

- Professor Richard Falk, Vice Chairman, Albert G. Milbank Professor of International Law and Practice, Princeton University,
- Dr Kader Asmal, Senior Lecturer in Law and Dean of the Faculty of Arts, Trinity College, Dublin,
- Dr Brian Bercusson, Lecturer in Laws, Queen Mary College, University of London,
- Professor Géraud de la Pradelle, Professor of Private Law, University of Paris, and
- Professor Stefan Wild, Professor of Semitic Languages and Islamic Studies, University of Bonn.

The commission toured the area of fighting and examined witnesses in Lebanon, Israel, Jordan, Syria, UK, and Norway. The government of Israel refused to cooperate. The commission's report, *Israel in Lebanon,* concluded that:

1. The government of Israel has committed acts of aggression contrary to international law.

2. The Israeli armed forces have made use of weapons or methods of warfare forbidden in international law, including the laws of war.
3. Israel has subjected prisoners to treatment forbidden by international law, including inhuman and degrading treatment. In addition, there has been a violation of international law arising out of a denial of prisoner-of-war status to Palestinian prisoners or detainees.
4. There has been deliberate or indiscriminate or reckless bombardment of a civilian character, of hospitals, schools, and other nonmilitary targets.
5. There has been systematic bombardment and other destruction of towns, cities, villages, and refugee camps.
6. The acts of the Israeli armed forces have caused the dispersal, deportation and ill-treatment of populations, in violation of international law.
7. The government of Israel has no valid reasons under international law for its invasion of the Lebanon, for the manner in which it conducted hostilities or for its actions as an occupying force.
8. The Israeli authorities or forces were involved directly or indirectly in the massacres and other killings that have been reported to have been carried out by Lebanese militiamen in the refugee camps of Sabra and Chatila in the Beirut area between 16 and 18 September.

Kahan commission report

See also: Kahan Commission

300,000 demonstrating Israelis put pressure on their government to investigate on the massacre. The Kahan Commission concluded in February 1983 that Israel bore part of the "indirect responsibility" for the massacres, advised Minister of Defense Ariel Sharon to be dismissed from his post and not to hold public office again.

Israeli population demands investigation

In its initial statements, the Israeli government declared that those critics who regarded the IDF as having responsibility for the events at Sabra and Shatila were guilty of "a blood libel against the Jewish state and its Government." However, as the news of the massacre spread around the world, the controversy grew, and on September 25, 300,000 Israelis—roughly one-tenth of the country's population at the time—demonstrated in Tel Aviv demanding answers. The protest, known in Israel as the "400,000 protest" (the number of protesters was first exaggerated) was one of the biggest in Israel's history.

Israel "indirect responsibility"

On September 28, the Israeli Government resolved to establish a Commission of Inquiry, which was led by former Supreme Court Justice Yitzhak Kahan. The report included evidence from Israeli army personnel, as well as political figures and Phalangist officers. In the report, published in February 1983, the Kahan Commission stated that there was no evidence that Israeli units took direct part in the massacre and that it was the "direct responsibility of Phalangists." However, the Commission recorded that Israeli military personnel were aware that a massacre was in progress without taking serious steps to stop it, and that reports of a massacre in progress were made to senior Israeli officers and even to an Israeli cabinet minister; it therefore regarded Israel as bearing part of the "indirect responsibility."

Sharon "personal responsibility"

The Kahan commission found that Ariel Sharon "bears personal responsibility", recommended his dismissal from the post of Defense Minister and concluded that Sharon should not hold public office again, stating that:

It is our view that responsibility is to be imputed to the minister of defense for having disregarded the prospect of acts of vengeance and bloodshed by the Phalangists against the population of the refugee camps and for having failed to take this danger into account when he decided to have the Phalangists enter the camps. In addition, responsibility is to be imputed to the minister of defense for not ordering appropriate measures for preventing or reducing the chances of a massacre as a condition for the Phalangists' entry into the camps.

At first, Sharon refused to resign, and Begin refused to fire him. It was only after the death of Emil Grunzweig after a grenade was tossed into the dispersing crowd of a Peace Now protest march, which also injured ten others, that a compromise was reached: Sharon would resign as Defense minister, but remain in the Cabinet as a minister without portfolio. Notwithstanding the dissuading conclusions of the Kahan report, Sharon would later become Prime Minister of Israel.

Other conclusions

The Kahan commission also recommended the dismissal of Director of Military Intelligence Yehoshua Saguy, and the effective promotion freeze of Division Commander Brig. Gen. Amos Yaron for at least three years.

Further opinions on Israeli role

Benny Morris, in *Israel's Secret Wars,* stated that Israeli forces provided the bulldozers used to bury the massacred Palestinians.

In the 2005 Swiss-French-German-Lebanese co-produced documentary *Massaker* six former Lebanese Forces soldiers who participated personally in the massacre stated there was direct Israeli participation. One of them said that he saw Israeli soldiers driving bulldozers into inhabited houses inside the camp. Another said that Israeli soldiers provided the Lebanese Forces soldiers with material to dispose of the corpses lying around in the streets.

Several of the soldiers said that they had received training in Israel. However, these claims are controversial.

Noam Chomsky and Robert Fisk have said that Israel could have predicted that a massacre by Phalange fighters who entered the camps might have taken place. In particular, such commentators do not believe it is possible that there were "2000 PLO terrorists" remaining in the camps, because (1) the Kahan Commission documents that the Israeli army allowed only 150 Phalangist fighters into the camps and (2) the Phalangists suffered only two casualties; an improbable outcome of a supposedly 36-hour battle of 150 militants against 2000 experienced "PLO terrorists" [FT].

International political reactions

The attack was explicitly grieved and condemned in Muslim countries in and surrounding the Arab Middle East. Many leaders from those countries urged the Palestinians to violently retaliate to earn sovereignty of their land. When Ariel Sharon had fallen seriously ill in January 2006, president Ahmadinejad from Iran reportedly referred to Sharon as "the criminal of Sabra and Shatila".

The attack was criticized by members of Western countries as well.

Opinions on Hobeika's responsibility

Robert Maroun Hatem, Elie Hobeika's bodyguard, stated in his book *From Israel to Damascus* that Hobeika ordered the massacre of civilians in defiance of Israeli instructions to behave like a "dignified" army.

Pierre Rehov, a documentary filmmaker who worked on the case with former Lebanese soldiers, while making his film *Holy Land: Christians in Peril,* came to the conclusion that Hobeika was definitely responsible for the massacre, despite the orders he had received from Ariel Sharon to behave humanely.

Sharon sues Time *for libel*

Ariel Sharon sued Time magazine for libel in American and Israeli courts in a $50 million libel suit, after *Time* published a story in its February 21, 1983, issue, implying that Sharon had "reportedly discussed with the Gemayels the need for the Phalangists to take revenge" for Bashir's assassination. The jury found the article false and defamatory, although *Time* won the suit in the U.S. court because Sharon's defense failed to establish that the magazine's editors and writers had "acted out of malice," as required under the U.S. libel law.

Relatives of victims sue Sharon

After Sharon's 2001 election to the post of Prime Minister of Israel, relatives of the victims of the massacre filed a lawsuit in Belgium alleging Sharon's personal responsibility for the massacres. The Belgian Supreme Court ruled on February 12, 2003, that Sharon (and others involved, such as Israeli General Yaron) could be indicted under this accusation. Israel maintained that the lawsuit was initiated for political reasons.

On September 24, 2003, Belgium's Supreme Court dismissed the war crimes case against Ariel Sharon, since none of the plaintiffs had Belgian nationality at the start of the case.

Assassination of Elie Hobeika

Elie Hobeika, the Phalangist commander at the time of the massacre, was assassinated by a car bomb in Beirut on January 24, 2002. Lebanese and Arab commentators blamed Israel for the murder on Hobeika, with alleged Israeli motive that Hobeika would be "apparently poised to testify before the Belgian court about Sharon's role in the massacre" (see section above). The Jerusalem Center for Public Affairs on the other hand suggests that rather Syria "might have been concerned where Hobeika's testimony could lead".

See also

- Karantina massacre
- Damour massacre
- War of the camps
- Lebanese Civil War
- 1982 Lebanon War
- Israel-Lebanon conflict
- Tel al-Zaatar massacre
- Hama massacre
- List of events named massacres
- *Waltz with Bashir*

References

- Bregman, Ahron (2002). *Israel's Wars: A History Since 1947.* London: Routledge. ISBN 0-415-28716-2
- al-Hout, Bayan Nuwayhed (2004). *Sabra and Shatila: September 1982.* Pluto Press. ISBN 0-7453-2302-2.
- Campagna, Joel (April 2002). The Usual Suspects. *World Press Review 49* (4). Web journal article, retrieved December 4, 2004.
- Chomsky, Noam (1989). *Necessary Illusions: Thought control in democratic societies.* South End Press. ISBN 0-89608-366-7.
- Eisenberg, Laura Zittrain and Caplan, Neil (1998). *Negotiating Arab-Israeli Peace: Patterns, Problems, Possibilities.* Indiana University Press. ISBN 0-253-21159-X.
- Hamdan, Amal (September 16, 2003). Remembering Sabra and Shatila. *Aljazeera.* Retrieved December 4, 2004.
- Harbo, John (September 20, 1982). Aftenposten. Middle East correspondent Harbo was also quoted with the same information on ABC News "Close up, Beirut Massacres," broadcast January 7, 1983.

- Kapeliouk, Amnon (1982). *Enquête sur un massacre: Sabra et Chatila.* Seuil. ISBN 2-02-006391-3. English translation available online here.
- Klein, A. J. (New York, 2005), *Striking Back: The 1972 Munich Olympics Massacre and Israel's Deadly Response,* Random House ISBN 1-920769-80-3
- Lewis, Bernard. "The New Anti-Semitism," *The American Scholar,* Volume 75 No. 1, Winter 2006, pp. 25-36. The paper is based on a lecture delivered at Brandeis University on March 24, 2004.
- Lewis, Bernard (1999). *Semites and Anti-Semites: An Inquiry into Conflict and Prejudice.* W. W. Norton & Co. ISBN 0-393-31839-7
- Mason, Barnaby (April 17, 2002). Analysis: "War crimes" on West Bank. *BBC World News.* Retrieved December 4, 2004.
- Benny Morris and Ian Black. *Israel's Secret Wars: A History of Israel's Intelligence Services,* Grove, 1991, ISBN 0-8021-1159-9.
- New "evidence" in Sharon trial (May 8, 2002). *BBC World News.* Retrieved December 4, 2004.
- Schiff, Z. & Ya'ari, E. (1984). *Israel's Lebanon War.* New York, NY: Simon & Schuster. ISBN 0-671-47991-1.
- Shaoul, Jean (February 25, 2002). Sharon's war crimes in Lebanon: the record. *World Socialist Web Site.* Retrieved December 4, 2004.
- Shashaa, Esam (no date).
- Tamal, Ahmad (no date). Sabra and Shatila. *All About Palestine.* Retrieved December 4, 2004.
- Tolworthy, Chris (March 2002). Sabra and Shatila massacres—why do we ignore them? *Global Issues.* Retrieved December 4, 2004.
- Transcript of "The Accused" (June 17, 2001). *BBC World News* (BBC-1). Retrieved December 4, 2004. **Note:** the BBC has a disclaimer that says "THIS TRANSCRIPT WAS TYPED FROM A TRANSCRIPTION UNIT RECORDING AND

NOT COPIED FROM AN ORIGINAL SCRIPT: BECAUSE OF THE POSSIBILITY OF MISHEARING AND THE DIFFICULTY, IN SOME CASES OF IDENTIFYING INDIVIDUAL SPEAKERS, THE BBC CANNOT VOUCH FOR ITS ACCURACY."
- United Nations General Assembly, A/RES/37/123(A-F). The situation in the Middle East (December 16, 1982). This version from UNESCO adds some footnotes missing in the General Assembly's original. Both retrieved 14 Feb 2006.
- White, Matthew (update July 2004). Secondary Wars and Atrocities of the Twentieth Century. Retrieved December 4, 2004.

External links

- Lebanese Civil war 1982 Sabra and Chatila massacre Pictures.
- BBC News archive and video.
- "Sabra Shatila Massacre Photographs, 1982." Archived from the original on 2004-10-09. http://web.archive.org/web/20041009202109/http://www.littleredbutton.com/sabra_shatila/.; archive is incomplete.
- "Eyewitness Lebanon." Archived from the original on 2004-10-09. http://web.archive.org/web/20041009200930/http://www.littleredbutton.com/lebanon/. An on-line book, with eyewitness accounts and photos from 91 international correspondents.
- Report of the Kahan Commission-hosted by the Israeli Ministry of Foreign Affairs.
- Sabra and Shatila by Robert Fisk.
- "Sabra and Chatila Massacres After 19 years, The Truth at Last?" By Robert Fisk, The Independent, November 28, 2001.
- Sabra and Shatila, the unforgivable slaughter (French).

Retrieved from "http://en.wikipedia.org/wiki/Sabra_and_Shatila_massacre"

Categories: Conflicts in 1982 | Israel-Lebanon conflict | Massacres of the Lebanese Civil War | Palestinian history | 1982 in Lebanon | Genocide

Hidden categories: Articles containing Arabic language text | All articles with unsourced statements | Articles with unsourced statements from April 2010 | All pages needing cleanup | Wikipedia articles needing clarification from January 2010 | Articles with unsourced statements from June 2007 | Articles with unsourced statements from January 2010

Chapter 14

The Sinking of the Ship Liberty

From the January 16, 2004, edition of the Stars and Stripes

A Fair Probe Would Attack Liberty Misinformation
—Admiral Thomas H. Moorer

While State Department officials and historians converge on Washington this week to discuss the 1967 war in the Middle East, I am compelled to speak out about one of U.S. history's most shocking cover-ups.

On June 8, 1967, Israel attacked our proud naval ship—the USS Liberty—killing 34 American servicemen and wounding 172. Those men were then betrayed and left to die by our own government.

U.S. military rescue aircraft were recalled—not once, but twice—through direct intervention by the Johnson administration. Secretary of Defense Robert McNamara's cancellation of the Navy's attempt to rescue the Liberty, which I confirmed from the commanders of the aircraft carriers America and Saratoga, was the most disgraceful act I witnessed in my entire military career.

To add insult to injury, Congress, to this day, has failed to hold formal hearings on Israel's attack on this American ship. No official investigation of the attack has ever permitted the testimony of the surviving crew members.

A 1967 investigation by the Navy, upon which all other reports are based, has now been fully discredited as a cover-up by its senior attorney. Capt. Ward Boston, in a sworn affidavit, recently revealed that the court was ordered by the White House to cover up the incident and find that Israel's attack was "a case of mistaken identity."

Some distinguished colleagues and I formed an independent commission to investigate the attack on the USS Liberty. After an exhaustive review of previous reports, naval and other military records, including eyewitness testimony from survivors, we recently presented our findings on Capitol Hill. They include:

- Israeli reconnaissance aircraft closely studied the Liberty during an eight-hour period prior to the attack, one flying within 200 feet of the ship. Weather reports confirm the day was clear with unlimited visibility. The Liberty was a clearly marked American ship in international waters, flying an American flag and carrying large U.S. Navy hull letters and numbers on its bow.
- Despite claims by Israeli intelligence that they confused the Liberty with a small Egyptian transport, the Liberty was conspicuously different from any vessel in the Egyptian navy. It was the most sophisticated intelligence ship in the world in 1967. With its massive radio antennae, including a large satellite dish, it looked like a large lobster and was one of the most easily identifiable ships afloat.

    - Israel attempted to prevent the Liberty's radio operators from sending a call for help by jamming American emergency radio channels.

- Israeli torpedo boats machine-gunned lifeboats at close range that had been lowered to rescue the most-seriously wounded.

As a result, our commission concluded that:

- There is compelling evidence that Israel's attack was a deliberate attempt to destroy an American ship and kill her entire crew.
- In attacking the USS Liberty, Israel committed acts of murder against U.S. servicemen and an act of war against the United States.
- The White House knowingly covered up the facts of this attack from the American people.
- The truth continues to be concealed to the present day in what can only be termed a national disgrace.

What was Israel's motive in launching this attack? Congress must address this question with full cooperation from the National Security Agency, the CIA and the military intelligence services.

The men of the USS Liberty represented the United States. They were attacked for two hours, causing 70 percent of American casualties, and the eventual loss of our best intelligence ship.

These sailors and Marines were entitled to our best defense. We gave them no defense.

Did our government put Israel's interests ahead of our own? If so, why? Does our government continue to subordinate American interests to Israeli interests? These are important questions that should be investigated by an independent, fully empowered commission of the American government.

The American people deserve to know the truth about this attack. We must finally shed some light on one of the blackest pages in American naval history. It is a duty we owe not only to the brave men of the USS Liberty, but to every man and woman who is asked to wear the uniform of the United States.

Admiral Thomas Moorer was Commander-in-Chief US Atlantic Fleet in June, 1967, when Liberty was attacked. He then served as Chief of Naval Operations from 1967 to 1970 and as Chairman, Joint Chiefs of Staff from 1970 to 1977. In 2003 he formed the Independent Commission of Inquiry with Rear Admiral Merlin Staring, former judge advocate general of the Navy; Ambassador James Akins, former U.S. ambassador to Saudi Arabia; and General Ray Davis, former assistant commandant of the Marine Corps. For complete findings and the sworn affidavit of Capt. Ward Boston, see The Moorer Findings at http://www.ussliberty.org/moorerfindings.htm

Events:

The National Security Agency recently declassified additional USS Liberty related materials. Unfortunately, they did not declassify all of the materials they hold. The redactions in the materials released are inexplicable, other than in support of the continuing cover-up.

On June 8, 1967, US Navy intelligence ship USS *Liberty* was suddenly and brutally attacked on the high seas in international waters by the air and naval forces of Israel. The Israeli forces attacked with full knowledge that this was an American ship and lied about it. Survivors have been forbidden for 40 years to tell their story under oath to the American public. The USS *Liberty* Memorial web site tells their story and is dedicated to the memory of the 34 brave men who died.

The Attack

After surveilling USS *Liberty* for more than nine hours with almost hourly aircraft overflights and radar tracking, the air and naval forces of Israel attacked our ship in international waters without warning. USS *Liberty* was identified as a US naval ship by Israeli reconnaissance aircraft nine hours before the attack and continuously tracked by Israeli radar and aircraft thereafter. Sailing in international waters at less than five knots, with no offensive armament, our ship was not a military threat to anyone.

The Israeli forces attacked without warning and without attempting to contact us. Thirty four Americans were killed in the attack and another 174 were wounded. The ship, a $40-million dollar state-of-the-art signals intelligence platform, was later declared unsalvageable and sold for scrap.

The Cover Up

Despite a near-universal consensus that the Israeli attack was made with full knowledge that USS *Liberty* was a US Navy ship, the Johnson administration began an immediate cover-up of this fact. Though administration officers continued individually to characterize the attack as deliberate, the Johnson administration never sought the prosecution of the guilty parties or otherwise attempted to seek justice for the victims. They concealed and altered evidence in their effort to downplay the attack. Though they never formally accepted the Israeli explanation that it was an accident, they never pressed for a full investigation either. They simply allowed those responsible literally to get away with murder.

In an ongoing effort to reveal the truth about the attack, the USS *Liberty Veterans Association* has filed with the Secretary of the Army in the manner prescribed by law a detailed, fully documented Report of War Crimes describing the circumstances of the attack on our ship and evidence that it was a crime under international law. In accordance with international law and treaties, the United States is obligated to investigate the allegations. So far, the United States has declined even to acknowledge that the report has been filed. The full text of the report can be found at http://www.gtr5.com/evidence/warcrimes.pdf

Anti-Semitism and the Anti-American Apologists

The USS *Liberty* Memorial web site abhors the racist and extreme positions taken by antiSemitic, Holocaust denial, conspiracy theorist and other such groups which often seek to identify with us and to usurp our story as their own. We have no connection with and do not support or encourage support from any of these groups including National Alliance, National Vanguard, The New Order, National Socialists, The French Connection, Liberty Lobby, American Free Press, Republic Broadcasting, USS Liberty Radio Hour, Storm Front or other such groups. We wish harm to no one and encourage social justice and equality for everyone; we seek only accountability for the criminal acts perpetrated against us and can do that without help from hate-mongers.

On the Israeli side, the group of pro-Israel, anti-American critics of our story, while small, persists in launching loud, vicious ad hominem attacks on anyone who attempts to discuss the deliberateness of the attack. These anti-American apologists refuse to discuss the facts of the case. Instead, they rely on propaganda and charge anyone who questions the Israeli position with being antiSemitic.

For detailed and authoritative accounts of the power and influence of the pro-Israel lobby, please see The Israel Lobby and US Foreign Policy by Mearsheimer and Walt and The Pro-Israel Lobby by Edward Herman.

The Betrayal of American Veterans

Americans who volunteer for military service effectively write a blank check, payable to the United States of America for an amount "up to and including my life." The United States, in turn, promises to spend these checks responsibly. That bargain implicitly includes a promise by the United States to protect them and to seek retribution against anyone who harms them. In the case of USS *Liberty*, the United States has failed to keep its end of the bargain.

Chapter 15

Conclusion

If you think this little book is about "Jew Bashing"; you're wrong. You've missed the whole point. This book is about getting to the truth, and it's about changing the mind-set of many different groups such as the Church, Congress, the American public, and special interest groups. More important, it's a challenge for a call to action to get enough people and organizations together to call for a meaningful change of the Israel/Palestine conflict that will cause Israel and Palestine to come to the table and carve out a lasting peace and an end to the conflict.

Israel/Palestine is unquestionably one of the most beautiful pieces of land on Planet Earth. It is a crying shame that there is so much pain, hate, and strife among the people.

My hope and purpose is to get inside the hearts of every reader to bring about change. A change of heart is what is needed. This can be done, and it will be done. It won't be done by summarizing each chapter into one sentence and calling that a conclusion. Rather, let me make a few suggestions that, hopefully, will cause you, the reader, to act.

Get educated. When I began writing this book, my main resources were books and firsthand observations by going over there again and again.

I read over one hundred books on the subject (both sides), and asked many, many questions from both the Israeli Jews in Tel-Aviv, Yaffa, Haifa, West Jerusalem and the Palestinian Christians in Bethlehem, West Jerusalem, Nazareth, Jericho, Ramallah and more. That's not a lot. It is certainly not enough to classify me as an expert on the subject, but it is enough to claim I am knowledgeable on the subject. Get educated. There are far more resources available today (The Internet; Google, etc.), than I had twenty years ago.

If you are willing to get informed, the confusion will diminish, and in time, you will be armed with the facts. The more informed you become the more easily you will be able to recognize what is truth and what is misinformation. Make sure your time is well spent by getting information from reliable sources. I have referenced every book written by every secretary of State of our U.S. government. Start with *"Politics of Diplomacy"* by secretary of State James Baker, since he is the pioneer of the peace process movement.

Inform your church. The church in America is an enormous source of strength and influence. The Episcopalian Church in America today leads the pack in their relentless pursuit in helping and supporting the Palestinians. The Presbyterian Church is second with all sorts of ways of equipping its' people to learn about the issues and sending and sponsoring members to go over there to be true ambassadors of Christ. I can't think of who might be considered third, but after that, most of the churches are clueless. Mainline Christianity knows nothing about the Israel/ Palestine conflict. The Christians in Palestine think the churches in America have abandoned them. The churches have not abandoned the Palestinians; they simply have not been informed. You can go a long way to solve this problem by informing your church leadership.

Go to your State representatives and inform them. Many are not informed. Your senators and congressmen can be faxed, e-mailed, have letters sent to them, and called.

You can give talks to schools, colleges, radio, and TV stations. Many of them are very open minded and willing to listen what you have learned.

Hit them where it hurts—in the pocket book. Urge our president to link human rights abuses to the amount of aid we give Israel. The U.S. government gives Israel billions of dollars of aid each year. If they would cut giving for each abuse, the abuses would go down real fast.

Get involved in your own community and make it aware of the issues. You will be surprised how much you can do and how much help you can be.

Finally, Israel has to demonstrate a true willingness to desire peace.

What must be done? For a start Israel can announce and end to all settlements. This will send a clear message to the world that Israel is genuine and its desire for peace. If not; anything they say is pure literacy.

If Israel truly wants peace; they know what they must do.

Resources and Citations

The Politics of Diplomacy
Secretary of State James Baker

The Mighty and The Almighty
Secretary of State Madeleine Albright

The Missing Peace
The inside Story of the Fight for Middle East Peace

Blood Brothers
A Palestinian Struggles for Reconciliation in the Middle East
Father Elias Chacour

They Dare to Speak Out
Congressman Paul Findley

By Way of Deception
The Making and Unmaking of a Mossad Officer
Victor Ostrovsky
Wikipedia
http://en.wikipedia.org/wiki/Sabra_and_Shatila_massacre

Additional references:

1.) Book Title: The Blood of Abraham,
Subtitle: Insights to the Middle East
Author: President Jimmy Carter:

2.) Book Title: The Lobby
Subtitle: Jewish Political Power and American Foreign Policy
Author: Edward tiznan

3.) Book Title: Special Trust
Author: Robert McFarlane

4.) Book Title: Faithful Triangle
Subtitle: The United States, Israel, and Palestinian
Author: Noam Chomsky

5.) Book Title: Whose promised land?
Subtitle: Israel or Palestinian?
Author: Colin Chapman

6.) Book Title: Armageddon Network
Author: Michael Saba

7.) Book Title: The Bible and Colonialism
Subtitle: Moral Critique
Author: Michael Prior, CM

Citations

Google

Wikipedia

Edwards Brothers Malloy
Thorofare, NJ USA
July 31, 2013